A GARDENER'S GUIDE TO

SOIL

Establishing healthy soil, for healthy plants

A GARDENER'S GUIDE TO

SOIL

Establishing healthy soil, for healthy plants

SUSIE HOLMES AND NEIL BRAGG

✠ THE CROWOOD PRESS

First published in 2022 by
The Crowood Press Ltd
Ramsbury, Marlborough
Wiltshire SN8 2HR

enquiries@crowood.com

www.crowood.com

British Library Cataloguing-in-Publication Data
A catalogue record for this book is available from the British Library.

ISBN 978 0 7198 4090 6

Acknowledgements
The authors wish to thank Louise Adams for the photos on pages 18, 34, 60, 72 and 88, Frank Ashwood for the photos on pages 64 and 65, Chris Cordwell for the photo on page 100 and the Royal Horticultural Society, Wisley, for the soil test documentation in Chapter 6.

Typeset by Simon and Sons
Cover design by Blue Sunflower Creative
Printed and bound in India by Parksons Graphics

CONTENTS

CHAPTER 1

UNDERSTANDING SOIL

The soil in your garden or allotment is your number one resource for growing plants, yet the importance of understanding it and improving its health is often overlooked. Having a knowledge of how your soil developed and its intrinsic nature will help a gardener to grow healthy plants in the best way possible. Many challenges to plant growth, such as adverse weather, pests and diseases, are less likely to cause major damage if the plant has a healthy root system – and a healthy root system can only develop in a healthy soil.

This chapter deals with how soils originate and the processes that are involved, because this will have a big influence on the type of soil in your garden. Resources for finding out more about your local soil types will be discussed and also the basic ways we describe soils and their properties.

How do Soils Form?

Soils have to start somewhere. The process of soil formation is very slow – it can take thousands of years for a few centimetres to form. Conversely, significant amounts of topsoil can be lost by erosion in only a few years under the wrong type of management. Looking after the soils in the world has never been more important and, even on a small scale in a garden or allotment, we can all do our bit.

Key Message for Gardeners

- Healthy soil means healthy plants.
- Understanding your soil and the life in it will help you get the most out of your garden or allotment.
- The soil is a gardener's most precious resource.

Soils, with the exception of fully organic (peaty) ones, are produced by the weathering and erosion of the local rocks (geology). The ease of weathering of the rock depends on its geological origin and the climate in the local area.

The weathering agents are moisture, temperature (particularly the extremes and range between freezing and thawing), sunlight exposure and wind. All rocks can be weathered and will erode; the speed of weathering obviously depends on the severity of the conditions the rock experiences but also the initial hardness of the rock. A very hard rock (volcanic in origin), such as granite, will weather and erode much more slowly than a soft chalk (marine origin), and the difference in the breakdown of the rock into its primary components will give the soil many of the properties that we associate with it. Considering how many different rock types there are, combined with different climates, it is not surprising that there is a large range

Rock erosion by extremes of temperature and the action of water and sunlight is the first stage of soil formation.

of different soil types both within the UK and globally. The first rule for a better understanding of your soil is to find what your type it is.

Finding Out About Your Local Soil Type

There are a number of approaches to learning more about the local soils in an area. One way is to find any geological survey maps for the location: for the UK and other some countries, this may be quite easy. The maps will usually show you the solid rock beneath your feet; however, the subsequent movement of material by ice, wind or water complicates matters so the type of 'drift' material overlying the solid geology is also important.

Ice

In the UK much of the country as we know it was – until around 10,000 years ago – inundated by snow, ice and glaciers, which formed part of the last major ice age. As a result, many rocks were transported by glaciers as they moved across the surface. When the ice eventually melted, it left piles of ground-up rock (moraine), which may not directly relate to the underlying geology. If you are on the Lincolnshire Wolds, for example, your garden

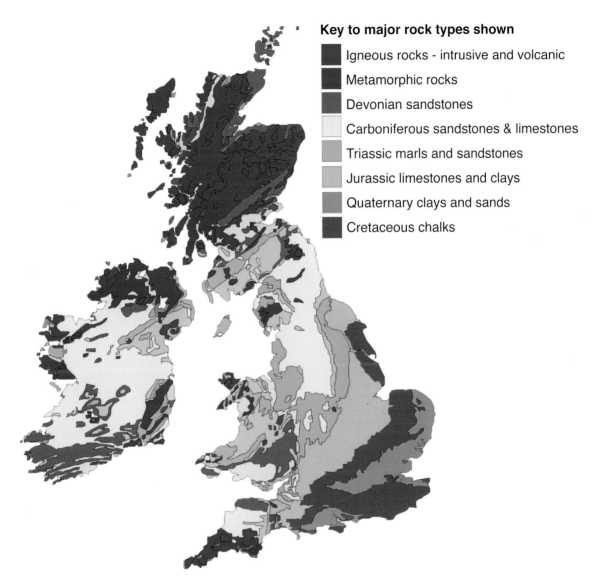

Key to major rock types shown

- ■ Igneous rocks - intrusive and volcanic
- ■ Metamorphic rocks
- ■ Devonian sandstones
- ☐ Carboniferous sandstones & limestones
- ■ Triassic marls and sandstones
- ■ Jurassic limestones and clays
- ■ Quaternary clays and sands
- ■ Cretaceous chalks

Simplified geological map of the UK.

may well be on chalk as the solid geology, but it is just as likely that in the valley bottoms and the flatter areas south of the Wolds, you will be on a mixture of ground-up rocks moved here from different parts of the country.

Wind

There are parts of the UK and central Europe where the main vector for soil movement was wind. For a sand to be wind-blown, the exact particle size is very important; given the correct conditions – for example, open fields with very little plant or crop cover – these particles can then be picked up by wind and deposited somewhere else. Specific areas of the UK such as the Vale of York, the Brecklands in Suffolk and soils around Western Park in Shropshire are dominated by wind-blown sands, which originated from somewhere out of the Ural mountain range.

The 'brickearth' soils of southern England are also formed from wind-blown sand, and these soils, combined with the local climate, were the basis for the development of the horticultural industry along the

Glacial moraines are the deposits left after the glaciers retreated at the end of the last ice age.

south coast of England. Well drained, and holding both water and air well, they can produce a longer growing season, so crops can be sown earlier in the spring.

Water

The final, and in many cases most dramatic, erosive force in the development of soils has to be water. From racing upland streams to peaceful meandering rivers, water is always picking up and carrying rock and soil particles. At peak flows, larger pieces of rock and grit are moved, while in the slower, quieter waters, the material carried will be microscopic clay sediment. As the speed of flow slows, particles carried in suspension drop out and are deposited – sands and gravel being beached ahead of the alluvial fans associated with river mouths – creating the mudflats of the river estuaries. Along all river courses there will be varying

Sands can be blown by the wind if there is little vegetation cover.

soil deposits and, because rivers go through phases of directional changes and rejuvenation, there may well be mixed deposits in quite small geographic areas

Ox-bow loops on the River Severn, Shropshire – an example of sediment carried along by water and deposited where the water flow slows down.

reflecting the river changes. This can lead to soils that in some areas are very clayey or silty sitting directly over sand and gravel deposits from previous river flows. The Severn River valley in Shropshire illustrates this very clearly.

Soil Maps

From the 1950s to the 1980s, the Soil Survey in England and Wales carried out soil surveys and mapped soils. When a 'new' soil type was identified it was given the name of the first place that the particular soil profile was characterized, and this was called a soil series. As an example, deep, silty 'Hamble' series soils formed on wind-blown fine sand deposits were first mapped around Hamble, near Southampton, but there are

Hamble series soils in other areas, such as Kent, formed on a similar parent material. The Soil Survey of England and Wales produced six regional bulletins with maps for the main regions of England and Wales. They are now out of print but may be found in second-hand bookshops. Some areas were mapped in more detail, down to county or even parish level (mainly in areas with important horticultural production), and such maps may be available via vintage map sellers.

Another useful reference is the Cranfield University 'Soilscapes' map from the Land Information System (Landis; www.landis.org.uk/soilscapes). This has digitized information from the old soil maps and maps of England and Wales into twenty-seven main 'Soilscapes', or soil types, with general information about the typical soil texture, drainage and fertility of each Soilscape. It is possible to purchase a 'Soils Site

Report' for the area around your postcode, which will outline the soil series in that area and their characteristics. It is important to remember, though, that in some areas soils have been disturbed or amended by previous land use so may differ from the original natural soils.

For Scotland, the James Hutton Institute has published soil maps for the main agricultural zones (mostly eastern and southern areas).

Table 1 Examples of some of the main soil types in the UK

Soil type	Examples
Sand	Suffolk heaths, Surrey heaths, Devonian sand, Vale of York, Western Park area of West Midlands
Silt	Lancashire coast, the Wash area of Lincolnshire
Clay	Essex/Hertfordshire chalky boulder clay, Northamptonshire
Loam	East Kent, Vale of Evesham, Sussex coastal plain
Chalk/limestone	Kent and Sussex Downs, Cotswolds, Lincolnshire and Yorkshire Wolds
Peat	Upland peat soils in Wales and Scotland; lowland peat fen in Lincolnshire, Somerset, Lancashire Mosses, Solway area
Man-made/brownfield soils	Areas restored after other land use; new housing developments with imported soil materials

Key Message for Gardeners

Do some research about your local soil types to find out their characteristics. The basic properties such as the soil texture (see Chapter 2) and chemical balance (Chapter 3) will have a significant impact upon what easily grows in your garden or allotment.

The Soil Profile

The physical matrix of a soil is made up of mineral particles of differing sizes, and these particles are split into three categories: sand, silt and clay. This will be discussed in more detail in Chapter 2.

Soils are, however, not just about the physical matrix but also organic components. These comprise not only plant roots growing into the soils, but a whole range of soil life including insects, earthworms and microbes (for example bacteria and fungi), which live in the soil and are responsible for the breakdown of dead and decaying organic material into the physical matrix. For a gardener, the key to a healthy soil is nurturing the life in it, as this will in turn create a good root environment for plants. This will be covered in more detail in chapters 4 and 5. A vigorous, healthy root system helps the plant obtain water and nutrients from the soil more effectively and fight off attack from pests and diseases.

The result of the breakdown of organic material is that the soil has a whole series of organic components added to it that help to glue or cement the physical particles together and result in what is termed the 'tilth' of the soil. The colour of the soil is a good key to how healthy it is – red/brown colours are seen in healthy soils because there is plenty of oxygen present whereas anaerobic, waterlogged clays tend to be more grey/blue in colour.

Soil tilth can be thought of in terms of the development of structural units in the soil profile. In a healthy, biologically active soil profile with lots of earthworm activity, the structure in the topsoil (A horizon – see below) will be formed of small units of soil, well rounded and with plenty of air space between the units for both gas exchange and water movement. This type of topsoil will create a good environment for seeds to germinate and seedlings to flourish. In a compacted or cloddy topsoil, seeds may fail to germinate if they dry out due to large air gaps and insufficient moisture, or rot off if the soil is too wet because it doesn't drain. Smaller seeds, such as lettuce, will be more susceptible to poor seedbed conditions than larger seeds such as broad beans.

If we examine a normal soil profile to 90cm (35in), what we normally see is at least three distinct, colourseparated layers or 'horizons'. These are normally labelled as the A, B and C horizons. A is called the topsoil and is normally the darkest colour with the greatest degree of organic matter and biological activity producing the greatest degree of tilth, and C is normally taken as the 'parent material' of the soil profile – relatively untouched by biological activity – although there may be deep plant roots and earthworm burrows.

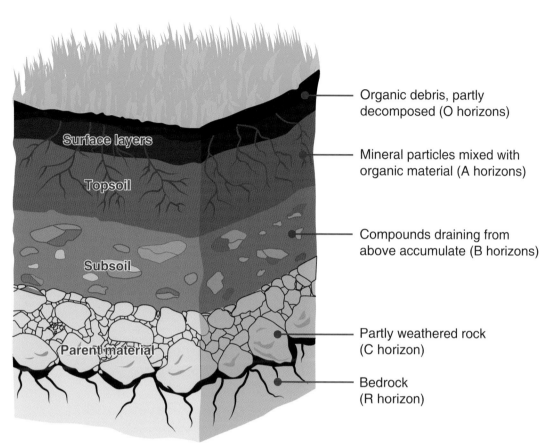

Typical soil profile.

Organic debris, partly decomposed (O horizons)

Mineral particles mixed with organic material (A horizons)

Compounds draining from above accumulate (B horizons)

Partly weathered rock (C horizon)

Bedrock (R horizon)

The B horizon, or subsoil, is the interface between the topsoil, where the main biological activity happens, and the parent material in the C horizon, so it shows some colour changes from the parent material and there will be some development of larger structural units. The structure of the subsoil will have a large influence on how well surface water drains through the soil profile. Even if you have managed to produce (or buy in) a well-structured topsoil, if it is sitting over compacted subsoil, rainfall will not percolate through and waterlogging can result.

Key Message for Gardeners

It is helpful to understand the nature of the subsoil in your garden as well as the topsoil layer because that will dictate how well the soil drains and if deeper-rooting plants, such as trees, will thrive.

Of course there are always exceptions to rules, and some soils will have topsoils with sharp angular structural units and be more of a grey to very blueish brown in colour. The B horizon in such profiles may have a distinct boundary to the topsoil, rather than merging with depth, there will be an obvious lack of earthworm activity and the structural units will be large and angular – and in the wetter months it may be impossible to see them clearly. The colour of the B horizon may be a contrast between blue/grey and bright red/orange on the cracks. This tends to indicate a very poorly drained soil, perhaps due to high clay content or a water table that is close to or fluctuating near the surface.

Soils that are naturally not well drained are better suited to long-term planting, such as lawns or meadow areas or shrub borders, rather than intensive vegetable growing. Many grass and meadow species can tolerate even some surface ponding of water over winter; they may die off but will re-shoot in the spring when the soil dries out.

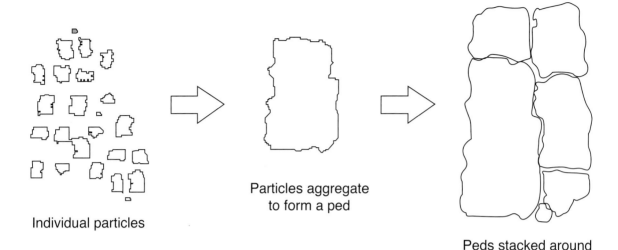

Individual particles

Particles aggregate
to form a ped

Peds stacked around
each other to form
soil structure

Soil structural units.

Key Message for Gardeners

If your soil has a naturally weak or compacted structure the drainage will probably be poorer and plants that do not tolerate these conditions may struggle even if you can improve it, especially if you are in a higher rainfall area. Try to choose plants that are adapted to your local soil type rather than battle against it – look at what is growing well in neighbouring gardens!

Organic Soils

The other great exception to the rule is highly organic soils, which may exist if the garden is in a floodplain or has a naturally boggy area or a spring. In these cases, any accumulating organic matter has no real chance to decay and the major biological elements, such as earthworms, may be missing. In this case the A horizon becomes a black accumulated mass of organic material – somewhat like a sedge peat layer. These soils are rare in gardens but do provide opportunities for unusual plantings of bog plants. The B horizon may be almost completely distinct from the A horizon – in some cases it will be alluvial silts and clays from the

floodplain. These soils will be naturally poorly drained and inundated with water for many months at a time.

Soils on New Developments

In many new-build housing projects the job of the garden development is contracted out. The original soils in the area will have been stripped prior to building commencing. The subsoil and topsoil often get mixed during this process and if the soils are moved when wet the structure is usually badly damaged so that even a good-quality soil can end up with compaction by the end of the stripping/storage/spreading process.

The result is that the plot of garden is often made up of a stripped material (parent material), which is then covered by an imported 'topsoil' from another area or manufactured topsoil. The soils are likely to have suffered from compaction due to movement and trafficking by heavy machinery. This may well mean that the soil in the new garden does not conform to any of the classic geological patterns described above and there may be a complete discontinuity between the imported topsoil and the underlying layers.

In such cases it may well be better to avoid traditional gardening practices such as double digging, but

Healthy, well-drained soils have warm brown/orange colours with lots of earthworm activity.

Poorly structured soils have dull brown/grey colours due to poor drainage and waterlogging, and little or no earthworm activity.

Bog garden plant communities thrive on waterlogged soils that would not be favourable for many other plant species.

Soils in new housing developments may be the ones originally present on the site or may be imported from elsewhere; either way, they are likely to have suffered damage to their structure due to movement and storage operations.

Raised beds are an option where the soil is very poor, badly drained or shallow in depth and are particularly useful for growing vegetable plants in allotments and community gardens.

to start initial planting in newly created raised beds or in containers while you gradually improve the soil. Container growing media are discussed in Chapter 7.

Summary

- Soils are generally the product of weathering and erosion of primary rocks, with the particles then further sorted by either wind or water.
- The soil in your garden is your number one asset, so finding out about the type of soil you have will help you learn how to manage it and keep it healthy.
- The health of the soil is related to the soil life and organic matter level and also the degree of waterlogging.
- Fully organic soils are rare in gardens but occur where organic matter accumulates under extremely waterlogged conditions.
- New house-build garden soils do not always reflect the original soil of the site, as these may have been stripped and then the garden landscaped to include an imported topsoil layer.

CHAPTER 2

THE PHYSICAL PROPERTIES OF SOIL

This chapter will cover the main characteristics of different soil types. It will also describe soil texture (the proportion of sand, silt and clay particles) and how this affects soil properties like drainage, and water and nutrient retention. We will also look at soil structure – the way the soil particles are aggregated – and how this affects soil properties and plant growth. The effect of poor soil aeration on roots and microbial activity will also be covered, as well as practical ways to improve your soil structure.

Once you know the basic properties of the soil in your garden you can make decisions about how to look after it. Some soils will need cultivating annually to grow crops like vegetables, even if it is just the top few centimetres; others should be disturbed as little as possible. The water-holding and drainage properties of the soil are closely linked to its type and will dictate issues such as which types of plants will grow best, if you need to consider a drainage system and how much irrigation plants might need.

We also need to think about the physical nature of the soil, not just as a home for plant roots but also as part of an ecosystem. A healthy soil that holds enough air and adequate water will provide a better environment for all the life in it, from earthworms to microbes, which are essential to help create a good soil structure. The best soil structure is made by nature, not humans.

What are Soils Made of?

All soils are made up of a mixture of mineral particles, dependent on the geology and climate where the soil profile has formed. The type of particles present and the amount of organic material will determine what type of soil a gardener will be working with in their garden or allotment. As well as the mineral component, there is a large living organic fraction in garden soils, described more in chapters 4 and 5.

Key Message for Gardeners

The physical and chemical properties of a soil are dependent both on the type of mineral particles present and the amount and type of organic material and biomass in that soil ecosystem.

Most of the soils in UK gardens will have had human influences on their properties. A long-established garden or allotment on what was once agricultural land will have very different soil properties from one on a brownfield site that has been used for building or a new-build site where soils have been recently disturbed (and often abused!).

If the garden is quite large, there may be more than one soil type present and/or different areas may have a different history, so it is normal to see variations in soil quality, especially if there are other influences, such as the slope and natural drainage. Other climate and microclimate factors – geographical location, the slope aspect, shade and trees that compete with your plants for water – will also have an influence on plant growth in the garden, but they are often things the gardener cannot change, whereas soil health can be improved. Soil health is all about thinking of soils as a living ecosystem and remembering that the life in the soil needs air and water as well as physical particles.

Solid/Air/Water Ratio

Just as important as the solid part of the soil (the actual mineral particles) are the gaps between particles

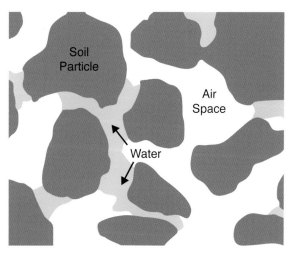

Large and small soil particles with large and small pore spaces.

because they will dictate the amount of air and water the soil holds. Air (oxygen) is essential for root growth and for many micro-organisms in the soil, and so is water. Air is held in the larger gaps between soil particles and also within the soil crumb structure. Water is held in the smaller gaps and also within soil aggregates. Smaller microbes in the soil live in the smaller pores in the soil where they get some protection from being consumed by the slightly larger ones (*see* Chapter 4). The amount of air and water the soil will hold is highly influenced by the types of particles it is made up of, and this is what is described by 'soil texture'. The air capacity of the soil determines how much oxygen is available for living organisms in it – less oxygen generally means less life.

The water-holding capacity of your soil will have a big influence on the types of plants that will grow best and how much additional irrigation might be needed, which is particularly relevant if you are growing vegetable or fruit crops in the garden or allotment – especially with the trend to warmer, drier summers in many areas.

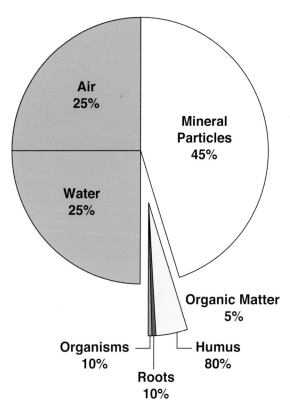

Pie chart of soil showing typical ratios of solid/air/water/ organic matter.

Key Message for Gardeners

Even if your soil has a naturally low water-holding capacity, adding organic matter over the years will improve this.

Soil Texture

Soil texture is about the ratio between large particles (sand), medium particles (silt) and very small particles (clay) in a soil. The proportions of each of these types of particle will determine the properties of the soil, although, as we will discuss later, organic matter can have a large influence on soil physical properties too. The nature of the particles present is obviously dependent on the underlying geology; a gardener cannot change this, but we can modify soils quite dramatically by how we manage them, for example by how we cultivate, deep or shallow digging and/or by the amount of organic material added. Methods for determining your soil texture are described in Chapter 6.

Any particle larger than 2mm (0.08in) is classified as a stone. The stoniness of soil is an important variable because a soil with a high stone content will hold less water than a soil of the same texture without stones. This is why digging grit into soil in a planting pit can help drainage (but only if there is somewhere for the water to drain to below). The type of stones encountered in the soil profile and how round they are indicate quite clearly their potential geological source and the degree of weathering by either water or ice.

The particle sizes in a soil also have a large influence on how water and plant nutrients are held in the soil. Soils with large particles (sand) have a relatively smaller surface area for water molecules and nutrients to stick to compared to soils with small particles (clay). Also with clays, there is what is known as chemical adsorption, which helps to hold specific nutrients (*see* Chapter 3).

As stated above, the large gaps between soil particles hold air and the small gaps hold water. Plants need both air (oxygen in particular) and water to survive, so a mixture of large and small pores, as found in a medium-textured soil, is the ideal scenario. Plant roots can grow through the large pores in the soil, but in a compacted soil, with little pore space, root growth will be restricted and therefore the volume of soil available to the plant from which to extract water and nutrients is reduced. The effects of compaction will be particularly evident if plants with a tap root are grown, such as carrots. If the tap root meets a compacted layer or a stone it will be misshapen instead of producing one long carrot or parsnip.

Note that in new-build gardens where a layer of 'topsoil' has been spread over the existing subsoil, there may well be compaction at the interface, due to the amount of trafficking that will have taken place during the building. In the first instance it may be

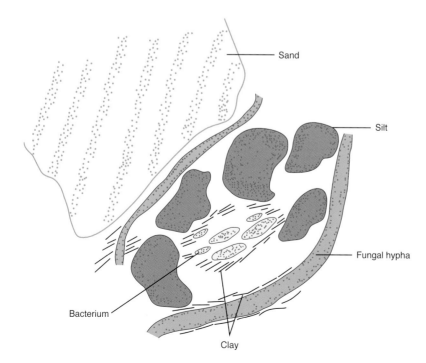

The relative sizes of sand, silt and clay particles.

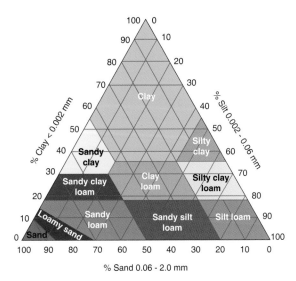

Soil texture triangle.

Soils are normally made up of a mixture of the three particle types with the texture name describing which are the dominant types present.

Soil Types

The main soil types found in the UK can be broadly divided into six main groups: sand, silt, clay, loam, chalk/limestone and peat/fen. In addition to this, there are manufactured soils that are produced by blending soil-forming material.

Sandy Soils

Sand particles are the largest ones texturally and are mostly the residue of the primary rock minerals, which are mainly silicates. Sand particles do not tend to pack too closely together due to their size and shape, which explains why sand holds a lot of air. Within this category there are coarse sands (the most gritty-feeling ones) and finer sands, much like with grades of sandpaper.

The coarser the sand, the larger the gaps between particles and therefore the higher the air-holding and the lower the water-holding capacity. A soil with a high sand content will therefore be well drained in winter but need plenty of irrigation in summer in order to sustain plant growth in dry weather. Sandy soils are not well aggregated and fine sandy soils are susceptible to capping over (when a crust forms over the surface), followed by soil wash and erosion on slopes if not protected by plant cover.

possible to simply fork down into the compacted zone to at least encourage some vertical movement of air and water; adding organic matter to the soil surface will encourage earthworms, which will start to burrow and create vertical channels.

Key Message for Gardeners

We can't alter the basic soil texture of our soil but we can improve the inherent properties by adding organic matter.

Table 2 General characteristics of sand, silt and clay particles

	Particle size (mm)	Texture	Water-holding capacity	Nutrient-holding capacity
Sand	2–0.06	Gritty	Low	Low
Silt	0.06–0.002	Silky	High	High
Clay	<0.002	Sticky	Medium	Medium–high

Table 3 The most desirable soil textures for gardeners/allotment holders

Texture	Characteristics
Sandy loam	Well drained but irrigation needed in summer
Sandy clay loam	Reasonable drainage and water-holding capacity
Sandy silt loam	Optimal drainage and reasonable water holding
Silt loam	Optimum water holding, good drainage
Silty clay loam	Good water holding, drainage may be slow
Clay loam	Reasonable water holding, drainage slow

They will warm up quicker in the spring than clay soils because they hold less water and will be workable over a longer growing season, which can be a benefit if you are trying to grow early or late vegetables. Being susceptible to drought will make growing moisture-loving plants such as roses, astilbe, hostas and hydrangeas more difficult, however, unless you apply large amounts of organic matter and mulches. Lawns and flower meadows will also tend to die off in dry summers without irrigation, but grass and meadow plants are adapted to this regime and they normally regenerate once rainfall increases, depending on your local climate.

Well-drained sandy soils are best suited to Mediterranean-type plants and herbs that need good drainage; if slightly acid, they will be perfect for acid-loving (ericaceous) plants such as heathers, azaleas, camellias and rhododendrons. With the addition of organic matter to aid moisture retention, they are also great for fruit crops, root vegetables and asparagus.

Sandy soils have a tendency to become more acidic (lower in pH) over time compared to silt or clay soils and have less nutrient-holding capacity, so lime application may be needed periodically and plants may need feeding more.

Sandy soils often show horizontal layering, reflecting how the sand was originally deposited by water.

Soil erosion by water leads to loss of the most fertile top layers of soil and causes environmental problems when sediment is then carried into water courses; it can occur even on very gentle slopes if soils are left bare during wet periods of the year.

Silt Soils

Silt is comprised of the finer resistant mineral particles – very fine sand and silt sometimes being difficult to distinguish in the field. Silt feels smooth or silky when rubbed between the fingers. The smaller particles mean it holds less air than sand but more water. Silty soils have the highest available water-holding capacity and also good nutrient retention so they can be one of the most productive soil types and can support a wide range of plants. They usually have a low stone content so are particularly suitable for root crops such as potatoes, carrots and parsnips. This type of soil is ideal for an allotment if you are lucky enough to have it.

Silty soils are often found in coastal or riverine areas, for example on alluvial deposits.

Silty soils are often the most productive and versatile.

Clay Soils

Clay particles are the smallest, and are too small to be seen even with an ordinary microscope. Clay is formed of very thin layers with an electrical charge, which nutrients and water can stick onto, and it has a very large surface area because of the layered structure. This explains why clay feels sticky when rubbed between the fingers.

Some clays have the ability to shrink and swell with wetting and drying cycles, which is why you see cracks in clay soils in dry weather. Clay will also swell and shrink when the water held within in it freezes and thaws, so frost can be beneficial to help break up lumps. When clay gets wet, it is easily compressed and the clods formed can be hard to break up when it dries so it is very important not to cultivate it or compact it when too wet (in a 'plastic' state). Although clay soils hold a lot of water, some of it is held so tightly by the clay particles that plant roots cannot access it. Clayey soils tend to be colder in winter because they are wetter, and the combination of cold and wet can damage some plant roots, particularly in more northern parts of the UK and Europe.

A soil with a lot of clay in is good for making bricks or pots but hard work for the gardener! The window when it can be worked is quite small – too wet and it will compact, leaving you with solid clods that are difficult to break down; too dry and it will be difficult to break up. The real key is to work with a clay soil, not against it. As already mentioned, some types of clay create their own natural cracking from shrinking/ swelling and freezing/thawing and this, in conjunction with pores formed by deep-rooted plants and worms, will create a natural structure. Digging will destroy this and hence clay soils may be best managed with a minimum cultivation or 'no dig' regime. Adding organic matter is a good way to make clay soils more manageable (see chapters 4 and 8). Earthworms are very good at creating burrows, which will improve the structure and drainage of clay soils naturally.

On a positive note, clay soils are less likely to become acid and they hold onto nutrients well, especially potassium. If the drainage is satisfactory, they are fine for lawns, borders and rose gardens. On an allotment they are best not disturbed at all when wet, so winter cabbages, for example, need to be planted out before they get too wet in the autumn and spring planting may need to be delayed until they have dried out sufficiently. Soils with a high clay content are less likely than sandy soils to be eroded if left bare, but benefit from mulching over winter to add organic matter.

Clay soils are described as 'heavy' soils and need careful management because they drain less freely than lighter soils, particularly if compacted by cultivating when too wet.

Loam Soils

Most soils in the UK are a mixture of sand, silt and clay, and this mixture is often called a 'loam'. A medium loam soil is the most versatile in terms of what can be grown successfully because it should have good water-holding capacity but also good drainage. This would be the perfect soil for a vegetable plot or allotment because it suits a wide range of plants.

Chalk/Limestone Soils

There are quite large areas of southern and eastern England (and northern France) that are formed over relatively young chalk or limestone deposits, for example the South Downs, the Cotswolds and the Lincolnshire Wolds. The chalk and limestone were formed when these areas were covered by shallow seas millions of years ago and are made up of calcium and magnesium carbonate from the shells of tiny marine organisms that lived in those seas. The flint found in some of these soils was also formed in these seas by organisms that extracted silica from the sea water to make their skeletons.

Sometimes there is a reasonable depth of topsoil and subsoil over the chalk or limestone but often these Soils are quite shallow. The difference between these and thin soils over other types of rock is that the chalk/limestone is more permeable, often with a lot of fissuring, which means that larger plants and trees can root into the underlying rock. This explains why large beech and yew trees can be seen growing well on apparently

Loamy soils have a combination of sand, silt and clay particles and are the ideal type for a vegetable plot or allotment.

very shallow soil. In some areas there are further deposits over the top of the chalk, such as the 'clay cap' found on the downland soils in parts of southeast England.

Soils formed over chalk or limestone will have naturally good drainage and are alkaline (high pH), which makes them unsuitable for acid-loving plants such as rhododendrons and azaleas.

Peat/Fen Soils

In some low-lying areas, such as the Fens of East Anglia and the Somerset Levels, the soils are formed over peat deposits and have their own quite unique character. Peat forms over thousands of years as the plant remains of mosses and sedges accumulate in stagnant,

Key Message for Gardeners

If you are on chalky soil and want to grow ericaceous (acid-loving) plants, they need to be grown in a container with a suitable growing medium because it is not practical to try to lower soil pH. You also have to be careful about the water used for irrigation. In a chalk or limestone area, the mains water may very well contain carbonates and therefore be 'hard' (as seen by your kettle needing descaling regularly!). If hard water is used on acid-loving plants then the pH of the container mix will gradually rise, to the detriment of the plant growth. It is better to use collected rainwater.

Chalk soils tend to be shallow and may contain a lot of flint; they are well drained but are naturally alkaline so not suitable for some plant types.

The Somerset Levels and other low-lying areas around rivers and estuaries usually have peaty soils that are water retentive and susceptible to waterlogging in winter.

oxygen-deficient water and fail to break down as they would in well-aerated conditions. This eventually leads to the accumulation of large deposits of organic matter, which is generically called 'peat' but which will vary in its properties depending on where it forms and how old it is.

In many areas of the UK and Western Europe peat bogs have been drained to grow food, for building and for peat extraction. Peat is a valuable carbon store, and there has been more emphasis in recent years on maintaining and restoring peat bogs to avoid releasing the carbon they contain into the atmosphere as the greenhouse gas carbon dioxide (CO_2). However, fully wetted ex-peatland areas do discharge methane into the atmosphere, which is a more potent greenhouse gas than carbon dioxide.

Peat soils are very high in organic matter and are often deep, but they are susceptible to wind erosion when dry and they are gradually shrinking in many areas as a result. Peat soils are naturally acid so need liming regularly to maintain a suitable pH for most vegetable plants.

The upland peat soils of the Pennines and the mountainous areas of Scotland and Wales are also formed over peat deposits, which form blanket bog in high-rainfall areas.

Manufactured or Imported Soils

With newer housing developments the underlying geology and local soil types may not be a good guide to what type of soil you actually find in your back garden. Sadly, developers do not always strip subsoil and topsoil under dry conditions and do not always store them properly. If soil is moved when wet and stored in large heaps it tends to become anaerobic and some of the soil life will be lost. Therefore, even if the original soil on site was of good quality, it is likely to have suffered from damage during the development process. In some cases the topsoil has been sold off-site and gardens may be mainly subsoil (or other mixed materials!), which are thinly coated with topsoil before turf is laid on top. Such 'soil' is likely to be of poor quality and to have been compacted by heavy machinery.

On some large sites, where there is insufficient topsoil for the gardens and green spaces, a manufactured

New-build gardens often have poor-quality soil, which may take many years to improve.

topsoil will be used. This is usually made by blending poorer-quality subsoil with green compost (made by composting green waste). If this is done well, a reasonable soil may be produced, but the site disturbance and movement of the soil can result in poor structure, compaction and areas of poor drainage.

Key Message for Gardeners

Even if your new garden has poor soil it can be improved, but it will take a bit of time so you can always start with small areas or some raised beds to get going.

Soil Structure

If you think of a soil as a house, the soil texture relates to what it is built from (brick, flint and so on) and the soil structure is how those building blocks are held together to construct the house.

Soil structure can be thought of at the macro and micro level. The macro level would be the whole soil profile to a metre or more down, and the micro level is the top layer of soil, where we would find most of the organic matter, the soil life and the plant roots. A well-structured soil has plenty of vertical pores formed by natural cracks and earthworm burrows in the subsoil, and a stable crumb structure in the upper layer.

In the upper layer of the soil, the microbial life and the organic compounds it produces can be thought of as the mortar or 'glue' that holds the particles together so the end result has some resistance to external forces (for example water). The ideal structure for a topsoil is one with particles that are held together in aggregates or 'crumbs' that are relatively stable – that is, not easily destroyed by water movement, cultivation, 'trafficking' of the soil with machinery or just by walking over it.

Once soil aggregates have been broken, any further rainfall will turn the soil to mud, and the process of aggregate formation cannot restart until that soil has dried out. Some soil types, such as sandy and silty soils, will then form a crust on the surface that rain cannot easily penetrate – such 'soil capping' is often

Key Message for Gardeners

Dry soils are much more resilient to structural damage than wet soils, so always try to avoid moving soil when it is wet. Allow the soil to dry out after the winter – in many cases not cultivating a soil until the end of March or into April will avoid any increased damage.

the precursor to soil erosion on sloping land. This is becoming even more of an issue with more extreme rainfall patterns due to climate change. It is estimated that more than 2 million tonnes of topsoil are lost in the UK annually due to water or wind erosion (UK Government 'State of the Environment' report, 2019).

One key measure to protect soil from erosion is to keep it covered – either with growing plants or a mulch. Using plants as a cover crop or 'green manure' is not a new idea but farmers are going back to these techniques as the interest in improving soil health increases. Maintaining plant growth for as much of the year as possible is also a way to maximize bio-sequestration of carbon – basically plants taking carbon dioxide from the air as they photosynthesize and storing the carbon in the soil. Soil holds around three times as much carbon as the atmosphere; UK soils currently store about 10 billion tonnes of carbon (Defra, 2009).

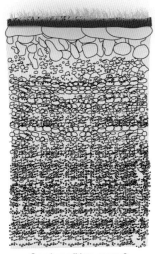

Good condition, score 2
No significant clodding

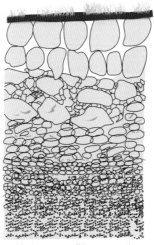

Moderate condition, score 1
Some clodding and fine aggregates

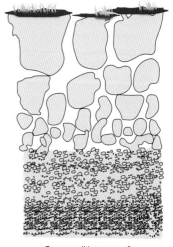

Poor condition, score 0
Mostly coarse clods

Good and poor soil structure.

'Capping' occur when the crumb structure in the top layer of soil is lost due to the impact of heavy rain and then this layer solidifies into a crust, which prevents water infiltration and leads to run-off and erosion. Capping can also prevent seedlings from emerging.

Key Message for Gardeners

Keep soil covered for as much of the year as possible to protect it from erosion, especially on sloping land. Additionally, a soil with a cover crop should dry out more quickly in the spring as the plants start to grow and transpire soil moisture.

Soil Structure and Water Retention

Soil water is becoming more topical in many parts of the UK (and other areas of the world) as climate change increases the trend to wetter winters and hotter, drier summers. Holding adequate plant-available water in our soils in the summer but also maintaining good drainage of excess water in the winter will be an ongoing challenge for gardeners.

Cover crops are used to protect the soil surface from rainfall, and they will also take up nutrients in the soil and act as a green manure when incorporated into the soil, particularly if nitrogen-fixing leguminous plants are included in the mix. Deep-rooting cover crops, such as oil radish, can also help to structure the soil and improve drainage.

Soil texture is the major factor influencing how water behaves in a soil, but the soil structure and the way soil particles are held together in soil crumbs or aggregates is also crucial.

The soil structure will determine if there are adequate vertical cracks to allow excess water to drain from the surface and into the deeper parts of the soil profile. If the surface of the soil is compacted or has a 'cap' on it, water will not infiltrate it easily and it will run off (on a slope) or puddle on the surface. However well-drained the soil is, if there is an impermeable layer deeper down or the ground water levels are high, water will not be able to drain away, so a low-lying area of the garden may always tend to be wet during wet weather unless raised beds are erected to artificially create better drainage.

Effects of Poor Soil Structure

A poorly structured soil that does not provide adequate pores for air and water and vertical drainage for excess water can become anaerobic (lacking in oxygen). Plant roots need to be able to explore a large volume of soil in order to access sufficient water

Poor soil structure is indicated by horizontal rather than vertical cracking and a lack of porosity.

Mottled orange and grey colours in the subsoil are an indication of seasonal waterlogging.

and nutrients, so a restricted root system due to compacted soil will affect plant health. Plant roots and many of the microbes in the soil also need oxygen for respiration. Mediterranean-type plants, such as lavender, are not well adapted to wet soil for long periods of time so are more suited to better-drained areas.

Anaerobic soils often have a 'musty' or 'sulphurous' smell because organic matter is not decomposed fully due to a lack of oxygen for the micro-organisms that are needed for this. Clay soils that are anaerobic will appear more grey/blue in colour rather than brown/orange and in some soils an orange mottling in the subsoil is a good indicator of conditions that are fluctuating between aerobic and anaerobic (for example if the soil is waterlogged in winter but dry in summer).

Key Message for Gardeners

Soil structure can be destroyed very quickly. Improving it takes time but it will help your plants develop healthy root systems and be more resilient to drought and pests/diseases.

Ways to Improve Soil Structure

The best way to improve most soils is to add more organic matter because this will feed the life in the soil (the 'soil biota') such as earthworms, which create channels, and the micro-organisms that help to produce stable soil aggregates. Ways of doing this in practice will be covered in more detail in Chapter 8.

Summary

- Soil texture describes the types of soil particles present – sand, silt and clay – and is predominantly determined by the soil type in your garden.
- Soil structure describes how the soil aggregates are held together and is partly influenced by soil type but also by how a soil has been managed and its drainage characteristics.
- Soils with good soil structure drain well; poorly structured soils are susceptible to waterlogging and will restrict root growth.
- The physical make-up of your soil (together with the local climate) will influence which plants will grow well in your garden.
- The soil's physical characteristics can be improved by adding organic matter.

CHAPTER 3

THE CHEMICAL PROPERTIES OF SOIL

This chapter will cover plant nutrients, how they are held in the soil and their function in the plant, as well as fertilizer types, the importance of soil acidity/alkalinity and the effects of waterlogging on nutrient availability.

Understanding which elements plants need to grow healthily and how these are supplied from the soil in your garden or allotment will help when deciding if fertilizers are needed. The acidity or alkalinity of the soil has a large influence on availability of plant nutrients; for allotments and vegetable gardens in particular checking the pH of the soil and adding lime if needed is important for good productivity.

Soil test kits for use by gardeners are available for do-it-yourself testing of soil pH and nutrient levels. They will not be as accurate as laboratory analysis but are useful for checking for soil acidity, in particular.

Nutrient Elements

Plants all require nutrients to grow. So far it has been identified that for healthy growth there are nineteen nutrients required by plants, including nitrogen (N), phosphorus (P) and potassium (K). These three elements are needed in relatively large quantities by plants compared to elements such as copper (Cu) and zinc (Zn), which are only taken up as traces by the plant but are still essential to healthy growth.

It is worth looking at the next bag or box of fertilizer bought for the garden as this will list the main elements it contains – N, P, K – and may then also contain a whole suite of elements in smaller quantities, such as iron (Fe), copper (Cu) zinc (Zn) and manganese (Mn). Sometimes on fertilizer labels, the elements N, P and K will be labelled as macro elements and the elements such as, Fe, Zn and Cu as trace elements or minor elements (this can be confusing as the latter implies that the element may not be so important). Whether the element is needed in large amounts (macro) or small amounts (micro), the fact remains that each one is essential for healthy plant growth.

Table 4 Essential elements for plant growth

Major (Macro) Nutrients					
Nutrient	Symbol	Source	Function	Deficiency symptoms	Toxicity symptoms
Carbon	C	Air (carbon dioxide)	Building of organic compounds	No growth	–
Hydrogen	H	Water	Building of organic compounds	Wilting/dieback	–
Oxygen	O_2	Water and air	Respiration	Wilting	–
Nitrogen	N	Air (legumes); organic matter; fertilizers	Building proteins	Poor growth; pale leaves	Dark-green soft growth
Phosphorus	P	Soil; fertilizers	Energy transport	Stunting, poor flowers/roots; purpling of leaves	Pale young leaves
Potassium	K	Soil; fertilizers	Sugar transport	Older leaf margin browning	Induced magnesium deficiency
Calcium	Ca	Soil; fertilizers; hard water	Cell walls	Tip burn, blossom end rot	–
Magnesium	Mg	Soil; fertilizers; hard water	Photosynthesis	Yellowing of older leaves between veins	Induced calcium deficiency
Sulphur	S	Soil; fertilizers; air	Building proteins	Pale leaves	Induced nitrogen deficiency
Micro Nutrients (Trace Elements)					
Nutrient	Symbol	Source	Function	Deficiency symptoms	Toxicity symptoms
Iron	Fe	Soil; fertilizers	Photosynthesis	Yellowing of the youngest leaves	Very dark-green leaves
Manganese	Mn	Soil; fertilizers	Enzyme systems	Mottled yellowing of younger leaves	Black spotting on leaves
Copper	Cu	Soil; fertilizers	Enzyme systems	Pale leaves	Loss of growing points
Zinc	Zn	Soil; fertilizers	Enzyme systems	Pale leaves	Stunted growth
Molybdenum	Mo	Soil; fertilizers	Enzyme systems	Strap-like leaves	Poor flower and seed development

Plants need a balanced diet in the same way as do animals, and an excess of one nutrient can be detrimental for the uptake of another one.

Most of the nutrients the plant requires are gained from the soil solution bathing the plant root system. The main exception is the plant's requirement for carbon (C), which is obtained by absorption of carbon dioxide (CO_2) from the atmosphere, which is then converted into sugars in the plant cells through the process of photosynthesis. Photosynthesis occurs in the chlorophyll molecules, chlorophyll being the green pigment in plants. The sugars the plant makes by photosynthesizing are the energy supply that drives the growth of plants and effectively fixes the carbon from the atmosphere – this is why plants are so important in reducing CO_2 concentrations and helping to reduce the effects of 'greenhouse gas' global warming.

The other essential element captured during photosynthesis is hydrogen (H); this comes from the photosynthetic process of water (H_2O) being chemically split into its components of hydrogen (H) and oxygen (O_2). During this reaction, the hydrogen is combined with the carbon to form the sugars, and the oxygen is released into the atmosphere.

The other nutrients come mainly from the breakdown (weathering) of the rocks that have formed the soils, from the fertilizers added to the soil surface and from the addition and breakdown of organic materials added to soils, such as compost or well-rotted farmyard manures (FYM). Inorganic fertilizers added to the soil will usually be water soluble, and the nutrients are then readily available in the soil solution for uptake into the plants. Organic materials, such as manures, compost, seaweed, spent hops and leaf mould added to soils, need to be digested and broken down by the soil's fauna – for example earthworms and springtails – and then by the soil's microbes (fungi and bacteria), which then excrete the soluble nutrients once they die. For more detail on this, see chapters 4 and 5.

The majority of the plant's requirement for nutrients comes from the plant taking them up in the soil solution – this is known as the transpiration stream. The transpiration stream has two main purposes: to bring soluble nutrients into the plant, which are then transported to the growing points; and to cool the plant and avoid it being scorched by sunlight. If you look at the back of a plant leaf using a hand lens, you will find small openings, called stomata, which can be open or closed. As long as the plant has access to moisture, then in warm, light conditions the stomata remain open so that water can be lost from the surface of the leaf by transpiration and hence cool the plant. If the water supply is limited, the stomata close to preserve the cell structures; eventually the plant will wilt as a defensive mechanism.

Functions of Plant Nutrients

Nitrogen

Nitrogen is the nutrient needed by plants in the largest quantity because it is part of amino acids used to build proteins. The two simple forms that plants can use are nitrate nitrogen and ammonium nitrogen. Different species have different preferences for which they absorb more readily. Woody plants tend to be adapted to use ammonium more, while grasses prefer nitrate. Plants that grow in acid soils, such as blueberries, take up nitrogen mostly as ammonium. In a normal soil there is a constant conversion of ammonium to nitrate by soil bacteria as part of the nitrogen cycle.

Nitrate is very soluble and is quickly washed away by rain if plants do not use it, so it is important to apply fertilizers containing nitrogen only when plants are actively growing. 'Little and often' is the rule with nitrogen fertilizer. It must also be applied in balance with potassium, especially for flower and fruit crops, because too much nitrogen encourages soft, leafy growth rather than flower/fruit production.

Key Message for Gardeners

There are a number of nutrients that are essential for plants to grow but they can only take these up in the simplest forms, not as large, complicated molecules.

Key Message for Gardeners

Only apply high-nitrogen fertilizers when plants are actively growing in spring/summer because nitrogen is quickly lost from the soil by leaching.

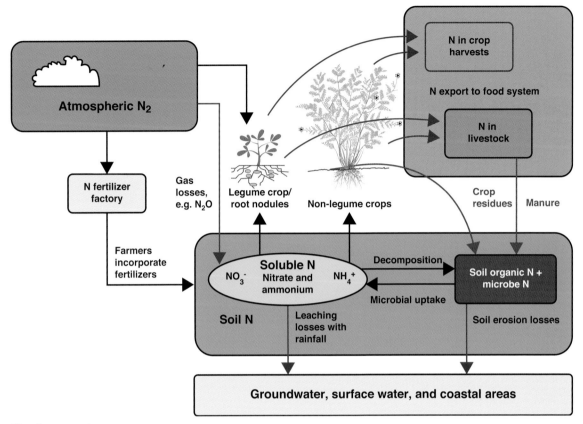

The nitrogen cycle.

A typical symptom of too much nitrogen being applied is that leaves are blue-green in colour, large and very soft. A plant fed too much nitrogen in relation to other nutrients, such as potassium, will have soft growth that is more susceptible to damage by pests and diseases. The plant will produce a lot of leaf growth but may not flower or fruit so well; therefore higher-nitrogen fertilizers are suitable for grasses and leafy vegetables such as cabbages but are not recommended for flowering or fruit plants.

Most lawn fertilizers are higher in nitrogen than the other major nutrients because it is nitrogen that will make lawns greener and more vigorous.

Phosphorus

Phosphorus is a key part of a very important molecule in plants called adenosine triphosphate (ATP). ATP is

essential for moving energy around the plant, which is why it is associated with good root development – energy produced in the leaves during photosynthesis needs to be moved into other parts of the plant, such as the roots. Higher-phosphorus fertilizers are therefore often needed for potatoes. Phosphorus is also a part of DNA, the complex molecule that contains the instructions a cell needs to reproduce.

Phosphorus in soils is mostly held very tightly in minerals in a form that is not available to plants. The only way most plants can get sufficient phosphorus in available forms (orthophosphate) is by forming symbiotic relationships with microbes in the soil, particularly mycorrhizal fungi (see Chapter 5). Only very sandy garden soils are likely to be low in phosphorus, so high-phosphorus fertilizers are not generally needed by the gardener (unless you are growing potatoes).

A ditch with an algal bloom indicating pollution with nutrients; this excess of nutrients, which disturbs the natural balance, is called 'eutrophication' and can occur in water courses, lakes and estuaries.

Even if symptoms of phosphorus deficiency are seen on the leaves (often a purple colouring of older leaves), this is usually a temporary uptake problem if the soil is too cold or too dry. Deficiency is unlikely in a garden soil, although top-ups may be needed on intensively cropped allotments. Applying phosphate fertilizer where it is not needed is bad for the environment because if soil particles with phosphorus attached to them get into water courses it causes algal blooms, which deplete the water of oxygen.

Potassium

Potassium is very soluble and is important for the movement of nutrients and water within plants. It helps keep plant cells plumped up, in particular the cells around the stomata (the tiny holes in the surface of the leaf through which plants release water vapour during transpiration). It is also important in sugar metabolism and hence fruit and flower formation, which is why it is recommended to use fertilizers with more potassium later in the growing season to encourage flower and fruit development. Crops such as strawberries will have a better flavour if a higher-potassium rather than a high-nitrogen fertilizer is used.

Potassium mostly occurs in the plant in soluble form and not as part of large complex molecules, so it can be moved around the plant to where it is needed. In the soil it is held on the surface of clay minerals so does not wash out of soil quickly like nitrogen unless the soil is very sandy; therefore the timing of application of potash fertilizer is less critical.

Many garden soils are well supplied with potassium; very sandy soils, however, tend to have low levels and potassium fertilizer may also be needed on allotments if a soil test shows a low level (for more information on soil testing, see Chapter 6).

Calcium

In the same way that calcium is needed for bones for structural support in animal skeletons, it is needed by plants to make cell walls, which are what keeps a plant rigid. It is taken up by plants passively with water, so if a plant is actively transpiring and taking up water through its roots, it will obtain a good supply of calcium. If the

Blossom end rot in tomato is caused by calcium deficiency, which in turn is usually caused by growing conditions, such as high humidity and lack of air movement, rather than actual lack of calcium.

plants are not transpiring (for example in cold, humid weather) the calcium supply can be interrupted and cause problems such as tip burn of the leaves and blossom end rot in tomatoes. Adding more calcium to the soil will not correct this. What is needed is a reduction in humidity to stimulate plants to transpire – for example by opening vents in a greenhouse.

Many soils in England are formed over calcareous rocks so have a continual supply of calcium as these are weathered. For acid soils, applying lime to raise the pH will also supply calcium.

Magnesium

Magnesium is central to the chlorophyll molecule, chlorophyll being the green pigment in leaves where photosynthesis occurs. Many garden soils are well supplied with magnesium so magnesium fertilizers are not needed, but application of excessive amounts of potassium can induce magnesium deficiency. This is often seen in tomato crops grown in grow bags where the regular feed is high in potassium, which then hinders the uptake of sufficient magnesium.

Sulphur

Sulphur is one of the major nutrients and is needed along with nitrogen to make amino acids and hence proteins in the plant. It can be deficient in the UK on sandy soils in intensively used allotments growing crops such as cabbage and onions, which have a high sulphur requirement (the smell of cabbage and Brussels sprouts is due to sulphur-containing compounds called glucosinolates).

Magnesium deficiency shows in the older plant leaves as a yellowing between the veins. Tomato plants often show magnesium deficiency when fed with high-potassium feed, as this interferes with the uptake of magnesium. The plant mobilizes magnesium from the older leaves to ensure an adequate supply at the growing point, hence symptoms are seen on the older leaves.

Minor Nutrients/Trace Elements

As the name suggests, these are the nutrients that are only needed in very small amounts by a plant but they are essential for many processes, such as production of enzymes (catalysts for chemical reactions). The most common reason for deficiencies of minor nutrients is a high pH (alkaline conditions) because they are then present in forms that are not available to plants. This is a particular issue with iron and explains why iron chlorosis occurs if acid-loving plants are grown on chalky soils.

Key Message for Gardeners

Nutrient deficiencies are often induced by the growing conditions or the soil pH rather than an actual shortage of the nutrient in the soil. Where intensive vegetable cropping takes place, however, as on allotments, the off-take of specific nutrients such as nitrogen, sulphur and copper may well exceed the supply capabilities of the natural soil and hence the need for increased fertilizer inputs, either in fertilizer or organic manure form.

Fertilizers

A soil analysis is useful to establish what type of fertilizer is needed for your soil (*see* Chapter 6). For many gardens, regular addition of organic materials will provide plenty of nutrients for normal flower borders and shrubs. The main type of 'bag fertilizer' that might be used during the growing season for faster-growing plants, such as lawns and vegetable crops, are high-nitrogen products but over-application should be avoided as it produces soft growth, prone to fungal diseases, and if it leaches into water courses it is very polluting.

There are basically two options when you are selecting fertilizers for use in the garden or allotment:

- Organic fertilizers – manures, composts, bonemeal
- Inorganic fertilizers – man-made bag fertilizers

Organic Fertilizers

Examples are animal manures (such as traditional farmyard manure or pelletized chicken manure), green compost, blood fish and bonemeal, seaweed products (for example kelp) and 'waste' materials

Iron deficiency causes yellowing of the very youngest leaves of a plant; it is often caused by high pH (alkaline soil) and/or waterlogging, and is commonly seen in ericaceous plants when grown in chalky or limey soils.

such as mushroom compost or spent hops from local breweries. When added to the soil, these materials need the soil fauna and flora to break the organic materials down and release the nutrients contained within them to provide 'slow-release' nutrients to plants. In other words, rather than benefiting the plant directly, organic fertilizers 'feed' the soil biology, which in turn adds to the organic matter in the soil, helping to stick soil particles together and give good tilth and at the same time releasing the various nutrients contained in the organic materials in a plant-available form.

The process of release of nutrients from organic materials is known as mineralization and is dependent on a number of factors:

- The soil pH being conducive to fauna and flora activity
- Moisture content – many parts of soil biology cease if the soil is too wet or very dry
- Temperature – the best activity range is between 10 and 25°C (50–77°F). Note in the spring soils can take well into April to reach 10° and if the soil is

waterlogged this can take even longer. Earthworms are a good indicator of soil temperature being at or near 10°, as it is then that their activity becomes noticeable.

Inorganic Fertilizers

Inorganic fertilizers are man-made ones sold as granules or prills or in liquid form. An example is Growmore, which is described as a 7-7-7 fertilizer. This is the internationally accepted standard for giving the nitrogen (N), phosphorus (P_2O_5) and potassium (K_2O) content of the fertilizer, as ratios. (By law, in the UK the phosphorus and potassium have to be expressed on fertilizer bags in the oxide form, not as the actual element.)

The fertilizer may also contain other elements such as magnesium, boron, copper or iron, and these would be shown after the NPK. Interestingly, Growmore was introduced during World War II as part of the 'Dig for Victory' campaign; its great advantage was that despite being applied at relatively high levels to the soil surface it would rarely damage a plant, as the available

There is a wide range of different fertilizer types available to gardeners.

nutrient levels are quite low. Other inorganic fertilizers include liquid feed products, often used for vegetables and crops in containers and grow bags.

Key Message for Gardeners

Use soil analysis to check if fertilizers are needed or not, particularly for intensively cropped areas, such as allotments, where nutrients will be depleted by crop off-take, each year.

It is recommended that when handling fertilizers gloves are always worn and hands washed afterwards. Some formulations can be quite dusty, so try to avoid breathing in the dust.

If there is no rain for a few day after a fertilizer has been applied, watering will help to get the nutrients to the root system.

Acidity and Alkalinity

The term 'pH' is used to describe the degree of acidity or alkalinity of soils, but it can also be used for any material or liquid. Lemon juice is sour – it is acidic – because of the natural organic acids it contains. Washing soda is strongly alkaline, as are all soaps. Liming materials, from chalk to hard limestones, are all alkaline in reaction and used to neutralize acidity in soils.

The pH scale runs from 1–14 with pH 7 being the mid-point, which is neither acid nor alkaline so is defined as neutral. Any number on a pH scale below 7 reflects increasing acidity towards 1 and any number above 7 towards 14 reflects increasing alkalinity.

Soils generally have an acidity/alkalinity between pH 4 and pH 8. Knowing the point on the pH scale where the soil sits is important, as this very much determines the natural availability of nutrients in the soils.

There are a number of easily available methods for soil pH testing. These vary from simple indicator strips

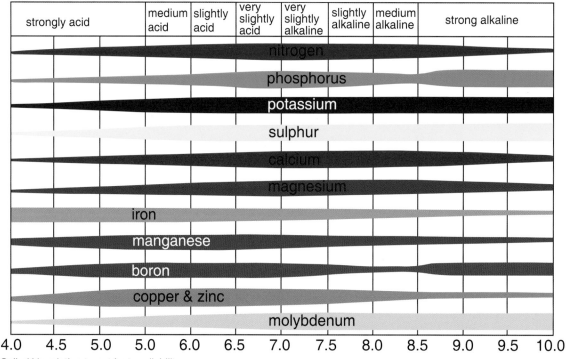

Soil pH in relation to nutrient availability.

to liquid soil acidity test kits and electronic soil probes, and will be discussed in Chapter 6.

As a general guide, the simple test kits based on colour reaction are perfectly adequate to give a general indication (unless you are red/green colour blind, as most of the simple colour strips and liquid are designed to turn red for acid and green for alkaline reactions). The problem with the electronic probes is that they are not stable in prolonged use and getting good contact of the probe with the soil sample can be difficult.

Correction of Soil Acidity

Soils that are either naturally acidic or have become so over many years of leaching by rainfall and nutrient uptake by plants can develop a pH somewhere between 4 and 5. When soils are acid, some elements such as manganese and aluminium become very soluble and can become toxic to plants. The disease club root, which affects plants in the cabbage family, thrives in acid soil, so maintaining a soil pH around 7 is recommended for vegetable plots and allotments.

Club Root

Club root (*Plasmodium brassicae*) is a persistent disease and, once in a soil, it can persist for twenty-five to fifty years without a host crop such as cabbage; the presence of freshly planted out cabbage-type plants can then stimulate it to reassert itself. It has been shown that the young brassica plants release compounds at their roots that awaken the resting bodies of the disease.

The aim with most soils is to keep the pH between 5.5 and 6.5 to optimize the overall availability of all nutrients. To raise the pH of a soil from the 4–5 range, ground limestone or chalk is normally used. A rate of between 200 and 800g/sq m (0.6–2.6oz/sq ft) will be needed, depending on how acidic the soil is.

Ground limestone can be bought from garden centres in small amounts (up to 5kg) and, for really large areas, bigger bags can be purchased from agricultural merchants. The best time to apply lime to a soil is in the autumn, then leave it or lightly rake it into the soil surface to be washed in by rainfall over the winter months. Never apply ground limestone at the same time as applying other fertilizers, as the latter can be 'locked' up by the limestone and hence lose their effectiveness.

The important thing to remember is that adding lime to the soil does not just neutralize any acidity but also supplies important elements such as calcium (Ca) and magnesium (Mg), which are not always included in other fertilizers.

Limestones are effectively an accumulated mass of skeletons of sea creatures that thrived in geological periods such as the Jurassic. The seas over this period were almost a 'soup' of creatures and the resultant deposits over millions of years have left the compressed and semi-hard limestones. The major chemical constituents are calcium and magnesium carbonates, which react with acid materials to neutralize the acidity and provide both calcium and magnesium, which are needed for the growth of all plants. As limestones are accumulated skeletal materials, they will also contain traces of many other elements that formed part of the shells of the ancient sea creatures, so they can be a good source of micro nutrients too.

Limestones vary tremendously in their hardness and reactivity. The white cliffs of Dover are formed of chalk, which is the softest geological deposit of limestone, while the material referred to as 'Shap Granite' from Westmorland is in fact very hard magnesium limestone – similar to much of the hard limestone found in the Pennine backbone of England. So, if you need a rapid rise in the pH of your soil, chalks will be your best choice; ground hard magnesium limestones will only very slowly correct any acidity.

Buffering Capacity

Soils derived from different rock types come with their own suite of minerals. Some rocks, such as those that give us sandy soils, are naturally very low in nutrients and tend also to become acid very easily as they cannot hold onto applied nutrients and liming materials. Conversely, clayey and silty soils have the ability to hold nutrients and take a long time to become acidic, as they do not lose their nutrients as easily as sandy soils and also have greater reserves of nutrients to start with.

The ability of a particular soil type to retain nutrients is termed the 'buffering capacity'. Soils with a higher buffering capacity are generally more fertile and plants grown in them will be less susceptible to nutrient deficiencies, so for vegetable plots or allotments it is good to increase it if possible. Organic matter can be used to do this, helping to improve the retention of nutrients in the soil and acting as a slow-release reserve of plant nutrients.

Waterlogging

In aerated soils, elements such as iron (Fe) and manganese (Mn) are in what is termed their oxidized state; this is reflected in the fact that iron oxide (Fe_2O_3) is the orange-brown colour of rust. Most healthy soils that are well aerated are therefore orange or red-brown in colour, although they may be darker brown in the surface layers due to organic matter incorporation.

When a soil becomes waterlogged, the available oxygen in the profile can be rapidly depleted by microbial use and by chemical reactions that reduce the oxides (chemical reduction). This does two things to the profile: the colour may change dramatically from the red-browns of healthy soils to blue-grey colours associated with reduced iron compounds; and secondly there may well be sulphurous smells in the soil profile, as there are a number of bacteria that can survive under waterlogged conditions of low oxygen and they use sulphur as the alternative metabolite.

Under waterlogged conditions plant roots soon fail; they require constant supplies of oxygen in order to grow. Reference is often made to rice plants and other

A typical 'brown earth' soil profile; these are mostly found in temperate regions and are usually well-drained fertile soils, so ideal for horticultural crops.

A 'gleyed' profile, showing the blue-grey colours associated with poor drainage in wet areas. Gley soils have a high clay content and are more suitable for grass and permanent planting than annual crops.

pond plants growing well under water; such plants, however, have specially adapted cells in their stems that transport oxygen to their root systems. Generally waterlogged soil requires land drainage of some sort; once the water level is controlled, oxygen can penetrate the soil and the healthy colours of oxidized iron and other elements can return. Beneficial micro-organisms will then return to the soil, as will earthworms and other larger soil fauna.

Summary

- Plants need nutrients to grow and they need them in a form that they can take up; the living creatures and microbes in soil play a key role in this.
- The major nutrients (nitrogen, phosphorus, potassium, sulphur, calcium and magnesium) are needed in larger amounts but the minor (or micro) nutrients are also essential for healthy plant growth.
- The soil pH (acidity) has a large influence on plant nutrient availability and liming of acid soils is important for maintaining soil fertility.
- Plant roots will be most efficient at taking up nutrients in a well-structured soil without issues like compaction or waterlogging.
- Only apply higher-nitrogen fertilizers in spring and summer, when plants are actively growing.
- If a soil has become acidic, lime it in the autumn and allow the lime to be absorbed into the soil over winter ahead of using other fertilizers in the spring.
- Remember that if organic fertilizers are used they need incorporating into the soil surface and the nutrients will not be available immediately – the microbes in the soil have to mineralize the organic material to make the nutrients available to the plants.

CHAPTER 4

ORGANIC MATTER

This chapter will cover the definition of 'organic matter' and 'humus' and how humus is formed. The effect of organic matter on soil characteristics such as water and nutrient retention will also be discussed, and why adding organic matter to your soil is a simple way to make it healthier. The carbon:nitrogen ratio of different types of organic material will be compared and related to how easily they are broken down by soil organisms, and how this in turn influences the composting process in your compost heap. The importance of the soil environment in the few millimetres around plant roots (the rhizosphere) will also be covered.

The answer to many soil problems in the garden is to add more organic matter to the soil because it will feed the soil organisms, which in turn help to create good soil structure and release nutrients in an available form for plant growth.

What is Soil Organic Matter?

Organic matter only makes up a small percentage of the soil as a whole (typically up to 5 per cent by weight for normal soils, although peat/fen soils contain much more), but it has a significant effect on its physical, chemical and biological properties. It is the food for all the life in the soil and, without it, soil would be inert

and plants would not be able to access the nutrients it contains.

The word 'organic' is confusing because it is used to describe types of farming systems that are based on principles of using natural inputs rather than man-made ones (or produce from those systems). In chemistry, however, 'organic' simply means containing the element carbon. In soil science, organic material is defined as matter composed of organic compounds that originate from the remains of living organisms or their waste products. The types of organic matter can be divided into these main types:

- Plant and animal residues at various stages of decomposition
- Manure
- Substances made/excreted by soil organisms
- Substances released by plant roots

The organic matter content of a soil can be measured by various methods, the most basic of which is weighing a sample of soil before and after burning it – because the organic matter will burn off, releasing carbon as carbon dioxide gas, while the mineral component of the soil will not burn.

The soil organic matter (SOM) level and the soil carbon level are related so SOM can be used as an approximation for soil organic carbon (SOC). Organic matter is typically 40–60 per cent carbon by weight. The carbon in fresh manures and plant remains is relatively available to soil organisms, but the carbon in humus or charcoal is quite inert and resistant to decomposition. Maintaining humus in the soil and conserving peatlands is important in relation to storing carbon and reducing carbon dioxide emissions and thus climate change.

Organic matter is depleted in the soil as microbes feed on it and the carbon it contains is lost to the atmosphere as carbon dioxide gas. This carbon dioxide gas is then taken in by plants as part of photosynthesis and the carbon becomes part of sugars and carbohydrates. This means there is a continuous cycle of carbon moving into plants and the soil, then being released into the atmosphere and passing into plants again. Without humans, the carbon dioxide levels in the earth's atmosphere would be gradually decreasing.

Humus

When gardeners talk about soil organic matter, they are often referring to humus. Humus is the product of decomposition of fresh organic material by soil animals and microbes. The nutrients in organic matter are not immediately available to plant roots until this breakdown has occurred because plants can only take up the nutrients in very simple form; large molecules cannot pass through cell walls into the roots. Humus therefore acts as a source of slow-release nutrients for

Key Message for Gardeners

Most soils contain large reserves of nutrients held within their mineral and organic components but the majority of these are not readily available to plants.

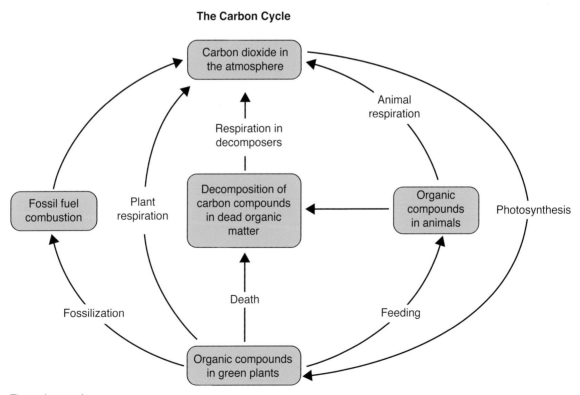

The Carbon Cycle

The carbon cycle.

both soil life and plants. It also increases the available water-holding capacity of a soil by acting like a sponge or blotting paper.

Most of the nitrogen in soils is organic nitrogen (it is attached to carbon in compounds such as proteins). It only becomes available to plants when it is separated from the carbon when organic materials are decomposed by soil microbes. This means the carbon cycle and the nitrogen cycle are closely linked.

How is Humus Formed?

The decomposition of organic material in the soil is dependent on the presence of soil life. The complex web of life in the soil will be covered in greater detail in Chapter 5.

Earthworms are sometimes described as the engineers of the soil because they drag organic debris from the surface down into their burrows and mix it into the soil. It is then decomposed by progressively smaller organisms. Pieces of organic matter are first shredded up by tiny insects and other soil animals such as mites and springtails, then fungi break down more resistant matter like woody material; and finally the smallest organisms (such as bacteria) finish the process. This decomposition requires moisture and oxygen so will occur quicker in damp, well-aerated soils and in warmer conditions. When soils are very dry and/or cold, biological processes slow down significantly.

A soil profile showing darker topsoil due to the presence of organic matter.

Geosmin

When rain falls on dry soil, certain microbes become active and release spores that contain an organic compound called geosmin, and it is this that causes the earthy smell we associate with summer rain on dry soil.

Key Message for Gardeners

Humus is what we call the partially decomposed organic matter found mostly in the top layer of soil, giving it a darker colour than the soil deeper down. It fuels many of the soil processes. Increasing the organic matter and hence the humic compounds in the soil helps to increase the aggregate stability of the soil and hence the tilth.

Benefits of Soil Organic Matter and Humus

The decomposition of organic matter to form humus releases energy, which feeds the life in the soil. In the same way as it is important for humans to have a large number and diverse range of microbes in their gut, it is important for soils to have good biodiversity. A healthy level of soil organic matter and humus has many advantages:

- Humus holds nutrients that plant roots can access over time and reduces the loss of nutrients by leaching due to rain.

- It helps with water retention so gives better drought resilience and makes plants less reliant on irrigation.
- While humus is made, the microbes release a sticky material, which binds soil particles together to make them more resilient to damage.
- It makes soils darker in colour, so they absorb energy from the sun better and warm up quicker in the spring.

Why do Soil Organic Matter Levels Fall?

If we keep growing plants in soil and then removing crops without replacing the carbon that they contain, soil organic matter levels will gradually reduce. This explains why organic matter levels in agricultural soils in the UK and many other countries are falling. Inorganic fertilizers increase the yield of crops but they are not replacing soil carbon, and crop residues, such as straw, are often removed.

In traditional crop rotations, grass or green manures are grown in the rotation as well as food crops and this helps to maintain soil carbon levels. Mixed farming systems, where animal manures are applied to the soil, can also help to do this. In continuous arable systems there is little return of organic material to soils, hence soil organic matter levels will gradually fall, especially if the soil is deep cultivated regularly. Likewise, on an allotment, if manure or compost is not added, the soil organic matter level will slowly decline, particularly if the soil is a lighter, sandy-textured soil.

Organic matter is also lost when we cultivate soils. Breaking up soil increases oxygen levels, which speeds up microbial activity and also makes it easier for microbes to reach organic matter held within soil particles. It also destroys earthworm channels and the network of tiny threads made by soil fungi and stimulates bacteria to break down organic matter. Ploughing or digging over soil is a good way to bury weeds but is one of the worst things for the life in your soil.

Furthermore, excess cultivation of the soil by digging or rotavating dramatically increases the amount of carbon dioxide emitted from the soil into the atmosphere, as the cultivation leads to massive peaks in microbial activity.

Key Message for Gardeners

Maintaining organic matter levels in your soil is the key to healthy soils. Try to work with the soil fauna, such as earthworms, and let them do the incorporation of the organic matter into the soil for you.

Carbon: Nitrogen Ratio

The main compounds in living organisms that contain carbon are carbohydrates and sugars. Carbohydrates are large molecules and sugars are smaller ones with the simplest sugar, glucose, providing energy for plant and animal cells. The main nitrogen-containing compounds in plants and animals are proteins, which are made up of amino acids.

Organic materials that contain a lot of carbon and not much nitrogen have a high carbon:nitrogen (C:N) ratio, for example shredded hedge trimmings, bark and sawdust. These materials are harder for microbes to break down than softer materials with a lot of nitrogen and not much carbon, such as grass clippings and manures.

Table 5 Carbon:nitrogen ratio of organic materials

Material	Typical carbon:nitrogen ratio
Sawdust	400:1
Bark	100:1
Leaves	50:1
Horse manure	25:1
Grass clippings	20:1

When microbes feed on organic material with a high C:N ratio, they use up available nitrogen and this can cause temporary deficiency of nitrogen for plants, causing them to look yellow. An ideal food source for microbes has a C:N ratio of around 30:1, which is why composting works best with a blend of woody (for example prunings) and fresh, nitrogen-rich material (for example lawn clippings).

If organic materials with a low C:N ratio (high nitrogen) are added to soil, more nitrogen is released than the microbes need so there will be plenty for plants. If a large amount of a high-nitrogen manure (such as poultry manure) is added, the microbes may release too much nitrogen, which can damage plant roots, especially young seedlings or sensitive plants such as azaleas or acers.

The Rhizosphere

When considering organic matter and the life in the soil, there is one area where most of the activity occurs. This is the layer of soil a few millimetres thick around the roots, especially the root tips, known as the rhizosphere. In the rhizosphere the number of micro-organisms is thousands of times higher than in the surrounding soil because this is their main feeding area. Plants release exudates from their roots, including sugars, carbohydrates and proteins, which the microbes feed on in exchange for their help with making nutrients more available for plant uptake. The level of fresh organic matter is highest in the rhizosphere because of all this activity. In addition, as root hairs and root cells die and are replaced, they also provide food for microbes.

The soil pH in the rhizosphere is lower (more acidic) than the surrounding soil because the plant roots release acids, and carbon dioxide produced by respiration forms carbonic acid when dissolved in water. This lower pH in the rhizosphere helps to make nutrients more available to plants and creates ideal conditions for fungi, in particular. Root exudates also contain compounds to ward off competing roots and diseases. Plants can change the chemical composition of the root exudate depending on which fungi and bacteria they want to attract.

Increasing Organic Matter in Soil

Soil organic matter levels tend to be higher for clayey soils than for sandy soils and it is easier to maintain the level in heavier clay soils because organic particles are protected within the clay aggregates and stick onto clay particles, making it harder for microbes to decompose them. In sandy soils, with their larger particles, there is less protection for the organic matter, so regular additions are needed to keep a reasonable level.

Organic matter may be short-term or long-term in its action, depending on how quickly it is decomposed. Short-term organic material, such as well-rotted horse manure, will be broken down more quickly and release nutrients faster, so will help feed your plants as well as build humus. Long-term, more resilient organic material, such as bark or green compost, may take months or years to release its nutrients but will still help to increase humus levels. Woody material will also encourage soil fungi, which are beneficial for the formation of stable soil aggregates.

The balance of soil fungi versus soil bacteria will be explored more in Chapter 5.

Key Message for Gardeners

It is beneficial to add different types of organic matter to your soil if possible, in order to give both short-term and long-term benefits.

There are two ways of adding organic matter to your soil:

- Mixing organic materials into the soil
- Applying organic materials as a mulch

Mixing

If you are using organic materials to provide nutrients for growing crops, mixing them in will speed up release of the nutrients. This is more relevant if you are using a manure or mushroom compost-type product, which is relatively short term. These products should be applied when plants are actively growing or about to start into growth, otherwise the nitrogen that is released will be wasted because winter rain will wash it away and into the drainage water (which is wasteful and bad for the environment).

Mulching

When using more long-term organic matter, such as leaf mould, bark or green compost, decomposition and hence nutrient release will be slower, and this type of product is often used to protect the soil over winter and retain moisture during the spring/summer. Mulching is also a good way of suppressing weeds

Table 6 Types of organic material used as a soil improver or mulch

Material	Longevity	Nutrient content	Notes
Composted bark	Long	May lock up nitrogen initially; very slow release of nutrients	Good for mulching; pine and spruce bark are best, and good for decorative effect
Green compost/home-produced garden compost	Long	Slow-release nutrients	Use reliable source (BS PAS100) to avoid contaminant issues. Coarser grade is good for mulching, finer (less than 10mm/0.4in) is better for soil improving. Available in bulk bags
Leaf mould	Medium	Slow-release nutrients	Make your own in a cage, compost bay or bin bags
Spent mushroom compost	Short	Fast- and slow-release nutrients, high pH	Do not use around acid-loving plants
Digestate fibre	Short	Slow-release nutrients	Becoming more widely available from garden centres
Farmyard/horse manure	Medium–short	Nutrient release depends on age and type; some nitrogen lock-up unless composted	Most horse bedding is now sawdust/woodchip, not straw. Herbicide contamination is possible if horses were fed hay treated with weedkiller

without digging if the mulch particles are too coarse for weed seeds to germinate. Earthworms will do the work of mixing the material in for you.

You will find that after you have carefully spread your mulch neatly over the bed birds will quickly redistribute it more widely, but that is a good sign as it means they are finding worms and other insects!

Types of Organic Matter

Note: Peat is not a good soil improver as it will be decomposed very quickly once mixed with soil so only has a short-term effect. Using peat bales, peat grow bags or peat multi-purpose compost as a soil improver is not recommended. It is also not a renewable resource, so it is wasteful to use for this purpose.

Composted Bark

Bark is high in lignin, the complex organic polymer that is important in the formation of cell walls. It is harder for microbes to break down so is a type of slow-release organic matter. It is useful as a mulch to aid long-term suppression of weed growth, conservation of soil moisture and winter protection around plant roots.

Bark mulch is a useful material to suppress weeds and retain soil moisture; different types of bark can be used, including long-lasting decorative bark chips.

Bagged bark chippings are available from garden centres and are particularly useful for decorative areas.

Garden Compost

If you have a larger garden that produces quite a lot of prunings and hedge clippings, you can make your own wood waste mulch using a shredder. Electric ones can deal with small branches, but for chunkier pieces it is better to hire a heavier-duty petrol-fuelled shredder. This shredded material can also be used in layers with softer material, such as weeds and grass clippings, to make garden compost.

Green Compost

If you do not have the time or space to make your own garden compost you can buy it, from the local composting site, a garden centre or garden-supply companies.

Green compost, or composted green waste, is made commercially by companies that take in green waste from gardeners, nurseries and landscapers and compost it. The quality of the end product depends on the type of material used (and how free it is of contaminants) and how well it is composted and graded, hence can be quite variable. It is an excellent soil improver, but it is important to make sure it is good quality, as sadly not all composting operations are as careful as others about keeping contaminants such as plastic and herbicide-treated lawn clippings out of their feedstocks. As a minimum, make sure the compost complies with Publicly Available Specification (PAS) 100. There is information about this from WRAP (Waste and Resources Action Programme). It basically means that the composter has followed certain procedures when making the compost.

One of the biggest concerns with compost (and some manures) is persistent weedkillers (such as those used by gardeners, farmers and grounds maintenance companies on grass to control weeds), which occasionally get through the composting process and unsurprisingly are very damaging to plants. Examples of particularly affected plants are tomatoes, potatoes, peas, beans, fruit trees, roses, delphiniums and dahlias; *see* the manures section below.

Leaf Mould

If you have deciduous trees in or around the garden, collecting the leaves in the autumn to make leaf mould is not difficult. The leaves can either be put into a leaf mould cage or into plastic bin bags and left to

Coarser grades of green compost can be used as a mulch and this will also supply slow-release nutrients to plants.

Green compost is produced from green waste collected at local authority and private composting sites and is widely available in smaller bags and semi-bulk bags as a useful material to increase soil organic matter levels. The quality of the end product can vary between sites so it is important to check that the compost at least meets the PAS100 standard.

Beech leaves are particularly good for making leaf mould within a year, as are oak, hornbeam, cherry, poplar and willow. Tougher leaves, such as horse chestnut and sycamore, need to be chopped with a shredder or mower first and can take eighteen months to two years to break down properly.

decompose. Softer leaves, such as beech, birch, hornbeam, oak, poplar and willow, will break down within a year. Larger, tougher leaves, such as horse chestnut, will take longer and may need shredding first for quicker results. If you use bin bags, add some water if the leaves are very dry and make some air holes in the sides of the bag. Good leaf mould can be used as part of a growing medium as well as a source of organic matter for the soil.

Spent Mushroom Compost

There are fewer mushroom growers in the UK than there used to be, but it is possible to buy mushroom compost from garden centres or bulk suppliers and it is a good source of organic matter when used as either a soil improver or a mulch. It is a mixture of manure and mushroom casing (often peat) with added lime so is quite alkaline (high in pH) and therefore not suitable for use around acid-loving plants. It also has a high nutrient content so needs to be well mixed with soil around sensitive and young plants.

Mushroom compost is particularly useful for vegetable beds and allotments because maintaining a good soil pH is important to help reduce club root disease in crops like cabbage and kale.

Digestate Fibre

There are now many anaerobic digestion units around the UK; these are used to digest organic materials to produce methane gas, which is then used to make electricity. They work a bit like a huge cow's stomach – bacteria break down the organic material (maize, straw, grass, vegetable waste and so on) and produce methane in the absence of oxygen (hence 'anaerobic'). Some crops are grown specifically to feed the digesters as a way of producing renewable energy.

The digester 'waste' produced by the process is separated into a liquid and a solid fraction. Most of the nutrients are in the liquid part and this is applied as a fertilizer on agricultural land. The dry part is a fibrous material that is now sold in some garden centres as a soil improver/mulch. It is not as long-lasting as more woody material but is still a good source of organic matter.

Anaerobic digestate fibre is becoming widely available and can be used as a mulch and soil improver.

Most horse manure these days is woodchip- rather than straw-based, and therefore has a lower available nitrogen content, but is a good source of potassium and excellent for adding organic matter. It is important, however, to make sure that the supplier is checking that the horses have not been fed with hay treated with certain herbicides.

Farmyard/Horse Manure

The nature of manure products depends on the animal species, the type of bedding material used for the animals and how mature it is. Cattle manure is usually straw-based but horses in the UK are more commonly bedded on wood shavings or sawdust, which are slower to break down than straw. Fresh manure has high levels of ammonium, which can scorch sensitive plants, so aged or composted manures are better. Manures are useful to provide plant nutrients, particularly potassium and also organic matter. Poultry manure is very high in nitrogen and should really be considered as a fertilizer rather than a source of organic matter because only small amounts can be applied safely.

If you are using horse manure, there is a slight risk of herbicide residues, just as with green compost, because certain weedkillers used by farmers on grass for hay/haylage can persist right through to the droppings excreted by the horses (they are bound to the lignin in the grass so are very resistant to degradation). The symptoms of damage are yellowing and cupping/distortion of the leaves and general stunting of the plants.

One way you check for possible weedkiller residues is to carry out a bioassay test with plants in a pot before you spread the manure.

Bioassay Test

1. Fill three 9cm (3.5in) pots with good-quality multi-purpose compost.
2. Fill three 9cm (3.5in) pots with a blend of one part manure or compost mixed with four parts multi-purpose compost.
3. Plant two broad bean seeds in each pot.
4. Water the pots and put in a warm place.
5. After the beans have germinated, any damage will be seen within a week or two.

Corteva (who make the weedkillers in question) have an advisory website with information and can provide advice if you think you have had plant damage from this type of herbicide.

Making your Own Garden Compost

If you have enough space, making your own compost is an excellent way of producing your own soil improver or mulch and is more environmentally

The symptoms of damage from green compost or manure containing herbicide residues are twisting and distortion of the plant; tomatoes and broad beans are particularly sensitive.

A garden compost heap is the best way to recycle garden waste into your own soil improver.

friendly than taking garden waste to the local recycling site in your car. It is easier to produce good compost with a larger volume because the temperature needs to get high enough for effective composting, therefore on an allotment it may be better to join forces with your neighbours. It does require some effort to make good compost, and turning it to get the necessary air into the heap is quite hard work.

Even if you are not able to turn the heap, if you use alternate layers of green and woody material and leave it long enough, it will compost down sufficiently to be used as a mulch. With regular aerating, it is possible to make compost in three or four months, but without this it could take several years. If the aim is to use the compost as part of a potting medium, it will need to be properly composted, sieved and blended with a low-nutrient material before use.

The Basic Rules of Composting

- Put the compost bay or bin in a shady area to avoid extremes of temperature.
- A bin/heap of at least 1cu m (35cu ft) is best.
- Use about one-third to one-half soft (green material) with the rest being woody (brown material).
- Shred larger pieces of woody material first.
- Turn the heap to mix in air once a month.
- Do not put grass clippings in from lawns treated with weedkiller.
- During dry spells, add water to keep the heap moist.

Worm Composting

Kits for home composting with worms are more suited to making smaller quantities of more nutrient-rich compost from recycling food waste and soft garden waste, such as weeds. The kits include the specific type of worms needed for this process (not earthworms) and it is important to follow the instructions to avoid odour problems. The compost produced will contain more nutrients than normal garden compost so is useful for digging into vegetable plots.

Green Manures/Cover Crops

Soils are healthiest when they have plants growing in them because they support microbial life and protect the soil surface from damage by rainfall. Green manures or cover crops are used between crops to provide fresh organic matter and nutrients to the soil, and can also help improve soil structure by creating root channels and taking up water from the soil. Cover crops can work well in large-scale farming systems. Farmers are encouraged to use them, particularly on lighter soils to take up the nitrogen left in the soil after harvest in the autumn and prevent it from leaching into groundwater before the following spring crop is sown. The cover crop also protects the soil from erosion over winter.

For gardeners, the main potential use for green manures is for vegetable plots and allotments, where there may be some areas used for spring/summer crops that would otherwise be left bare over winter. The problem on a smaller scale is they take effort to establish and can lead to carry-over of weeds or diseases to the next crop. They also need to be destroyed in the early spring, which means digging, and the moisture held by them might be a disadvantage on a clay soil so they are more suited to lighter soil types.

An easier way to add organic matter to your plot and avoid the hassle of planting a green manure crop is probably just a good layer of compost over the winter, which the worms will gradually incorporate for you.

Summary

- Organic matter is key for healthy soils as it is the food for soil life.
- Organic matter is also critical for good soil structure because it helps the formation of stable aggregates.
- Soils with good organic matter levels hold more water and nutrients.
- Cultivating soils speeds up organic matter breakdown, so minimizing soil disturbance helps to preserve humus levels.
- Different types of organic matter give different benefits to the soil, but nearly all soil types will be improved by adding bulky organic material regularly.

CHAPTER 5

SOIL BIOLOGY

Understanding what the life in the soil does and how it helps plants grow is essential for gardeners because it will do a lot of the hard work for us if we provide the right environment. Many of the creatures living in soil are too small to see with the naked eye but one of the simplest ways to diagnose if a soil is healthy or not is just to count the number of earthworms.

Microbes in the soil live in symbiotic association with plant roots, with both the plant and the microbe benefiting. Without the life forms in the soil (sometimes called the 'biota'), organic debris would just pile up on the soil surface and would not be incorporated into the soil as humus, and plants would not be able to access most of the soil nutrients because they would not be in an available form.

This chapter will cover soil life forms from the larger organisms (the macrobiota) to the smaller organisms (the mesobiota and microbiota). Mycorrhizal fungi and nitrogen-fixing bacteria will also be discussed.

Life in the Soil

Soil is a living ecosystem with a huge number and variety of organisms making it their home, from moles to bacteria. This life in the soil is crucial for nutrient cycling and decomposition of organic matter, and without it plants could not thrive. Soil is the life support system for human life on Earth.

All life on the planet needs a source of energy. For plants, this energy source is the sun, and they use the process of photosynthesis to make carbon compounds using the carbon dioxide in the air and water. Other organisms that are not able to make their own food in this way rely on eating plants. When living organisms die, the carbon they contain is used by microbes as an energy source and they then become the food for larger organisms; this is how nutrients are cycled and the biota in the soil are the key to this process.

Living organisms need energy, water and nutrients. As they process nutrients, waste is produced. Other organisms feed on smaller ones or on the waste products so there is not much 'free energy' in a soil ecosystem because the carbon is held in complex molecules, such as carbohydrates and sugars, which have to been broken down into simple forms before plants can absorb them. Most soil organisms are usually in a starved condition waiting for the next meal! If a food source, such as some compost or manure, is added to a soil, there is a sudden burst of life as organisms take advantage of the energy available.

Amazing Facts about Life in the Soil

- There is more biodiversity in the top layer of soil than anywhere else on the planet, but many of the organisms have yet to be identified.
- It has been calculated that, for arable land, there are around 2 tonnes/acre of living organisms in the soil – that is the equivalent weight of about four cows or horses on an acre of land.
- For grassland, the soil life is estimated at around 40 tonnes/acre (or eighty cows).
- In a teaspoon of soil there are more soil microbes than there are people on the Earth!

Table 7 Types of life in the soil

Macrobiota	Mesobiota	Microbiota
Mammals	Mites (Acari)	Fungi
Amphibians/reptiles	Springtails	Nematodes
Birds	(Collembola)	Protozoa
Earthworms	Water bears	Bacteria
Ants	(tardigrades)	Actinomycetes
Centipedes/millipedes		Virus
Woodlice		
Ground beetles		

Larger animals (the macrobiota), such as rabbits or birds, use the soil as just one part of their living environment, for example for nesting burrows. Smaller organisms (mesobiota and microbiota) spend all or most of their life in the soil. In the soil ecosystem the different types of living organism are all interconnected in a complicated soil food web, larger organisms feeding on smaller ones.

Earthworms

In many soils earthworms are perhaps the most important of the larger soil biota because they drag organic matter from the surface down into their burrows and start the mixing process. In acid soils under coniferous forests, mixing of organic material into the soil is carried out by a smaller type of worm, called pot-worms.

In some ecosystems, such as in the tropics, ants or termites carry out a similar role to earthworms, aerating the soil by digging tunnels for their nests and mixing nutrients through the soil.

Charles Darwin's book *The Origin of Species* is well known, but he wrote an equally important one about earthworms in 1881 – *The Formation of Vegetable Mould Through the Action of Worms*, which was actually his best-selling book. In it he said 'It may be

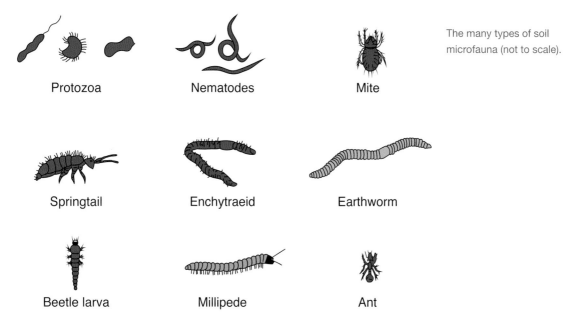

Protozoa   Nematodes   Mite

The many types of soil microfauna (not to scale).

Springtail   Enchytraeid   Earthworm

Beetle larva   Millipede   Ant

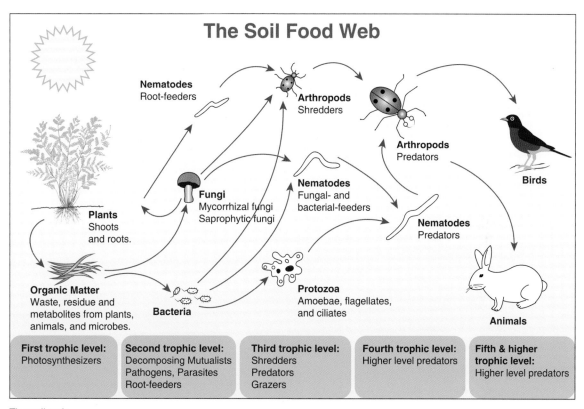

The Soil Food Web

Nematodes
Root-feeders

Arthropods
Shredders

Arthropods
Predators

Birds

Fungi
Mycorrhizal fungi
Saprophytic fungi

Nematodes
Fungal- and
bacterial-feeders

Nematodes
Predators

Plants
Shoots
and roots.

Protozoa
Amoebae, flagellates,
and ciliates

Organic Matter
Waste, residue and
metabolites from plants,
animals, and microbes.

Bacteria

Animals

First trophic level:	Second trophic level:	Third trophic level:	Fourth trophic level:	Fifth & higher trophic level:
Photosynthesizers	Decomposing Mutualists Pathogens, Parasites Root-feeders	Shredders Predators Grazers	Higher level predators	Higher level predators

The soil web.

Earthworms are a key indicator of a healthy soil and very important for mixing organic material into the soil profile and creating porosity with their burrows. The deep-burrowing ones can live for up to ten years.

doubted whether there are many animals which have played so important a part in the history of the world as have these lowly organized creatures'.

There are twenty-seven species of earthworm that are native to the UK, which fall into three main types, as described in Table 8. They all need moisture to survive so will tend to move deeper into the soil if it starts to dry out. Some live in the surface litter and others burrow deep into the soil.

Table 8 Types of earthworm

	Habitat	Size	Colour	Benefits for gardeners
Epigeic	Surface litter, compost; non-burrowing	4–8cm (1.5–3in)	Dark red	Breaking down organic material
Endogeic	0–50cm of soil (0–20in); horizontal burrows	2–30cm (0.75–12in)	Pale pink or green	Mixing of organic matter into the soil
Anecic	Subsoil –1m (3ft)+; long-term vertical burrows	>8cm (3in)	Dark red	Improving rainfall infiltration and aeration of the soil

Turning over the soil by digging or rotavating destroys earthworm burrows and is particularly detrimental for anecic worms because they create long-term channels.

Earthworm presence has been shown to increase crop yields and increase soil aggregate stability as well as water infiltration, so anything you can do to increase numbers in your garden or allotment will be beneficial.

Key Message for Gardeners

Try to do everything you can to encourage earthworms in your soil – keep adding organic matter, avoid pesticide use and minimize soil disturbance.

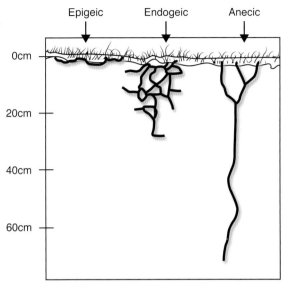

Types of earthworm and where they burrow in the soil.

Counting earthworms is one way of assessing the health of your soil (*see* Chapter 6).

One of the unfortunate consequences of importing plants from other parts of the world was the arrival in the UK in the 1960s of the New Zealand flatworm, which feeds on our native earthworms and has drastically reduced their numbers in some areas. They prefer cooler temperatures so are mostly found in Scotland and northern England. They are flat, about 10–15cm (4–6in) long, pointed at both ends, dark brown on top and paler underneath with a sticky mucous covering. They are most likely to be found underneath a plant pot or stone. There are other non-native flatworm species that have been introduced into the UK accidentally that also feed on our native earthworms, for example the Obama flatworm. If you suspect you have found a flatworm, the Great Britain Non-Native Species Secretariat website has more information.

Centipedes and Millipedes

There are many species of centipede and millipede that generally live in the surface layer of the soil. They vary from a few millimetres in length to 10cm (4in) or more. They have many legs, but not a hundred or a thousand as their names suggest! Centipedes have one pair of legs per segment and millipedes two pairs

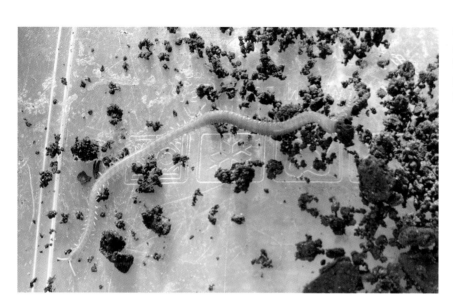

Centipedes live on the soil surface but also burrow in the soil and are natural predators of some insect pests.

per segment. These creatures are very important for eating dead plant material, so they carry out the first stage of decomposition, and were one of the earliest type of animal to live on the Earth.

Ground Beetles

There are also many species of ground beetle, varying in size from 2mm to 25mm (0.075–1in). They feed on insects and other small invertebrates in the leaf litter, the larvae living in the soil. They are useful predators in your garden because they emerge at night to eat pests such as slugs, vine weevil larvae and caterpillars. Beetles are used as an indicator of healthy soil because they are apex predators – if there is a large diverse population than means there is a good population of smaller invertebrates. Sheltered areas in the garden with plenty of leaf litter or compost cover provide a good habitat for ground beetles – another reason for using mulches and not having too tidy a garden.

Mites and Springtails

Mites are related to spiders but are smaller in size with many different types. Springtails are another group of soil animals that live either on the soil surface or below it. Both mites and springtails are key contributors to the formation of soil structure and humus because they feed on leaf litter and fungi in the soil and their faeces is a major component of humus.

There are thousands of species of mites and spring-tails – one handful of garden soil may contain hundreds or thousands of individuals from hundreds of different species. They are used by soil scientists as indicators of soil health – the greater the number of species present, the healthier the soil, particularly of the types of springtail that live below the surface of the soil, which are less mobile and therefore more susceptible to soil disturbance.

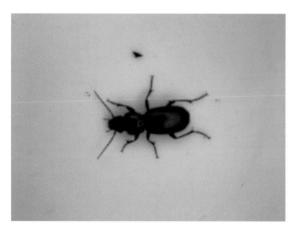

Ground beetles are friends of the gardener, feeding on slugs, cutworms, leatherjackets and caterpillars.

There are many types of springtail; they feed on decaying plant material, algae and moulds so are valuable in nutrient recycling and an indicator of healthy soil.

Soil mites feed on organic matter so are part of the nutrient cycling process.

Key Message for Gardeners

There are thousands of tiny animals living in the soil that are all necessary in the soil ecosystem and are working to keep it healthy. Adding organic matter and minimizing soil disturbance will help them.

Tardigrades

Moving on to soil life that cannot be seen with the naked eye but that is every bit as critical for soil health, we come to tardigrades (water bears). There are thousands of species on Earth, some of which live in the soil. Tardigrades mostly live in patches of moss or

Tardigrades or 'water bears' are tiny segmented soil animals, about 0.5mm long. They are almost indestructible and can survive extreme temperatures and pressures and even exposure to radiation. They can dehydrate themselves in drought conditions by transforming into a dormant form, known as a 'tun'. They feed on bacteria, plants or other tardigrades.

lichen and feed on smaller creatures. They are up to about 1mm (0.04in) in size with four pairs of clawed legs and look a bit like small bears under the microscope – hence the name! They are found in the most extreme environments, from very hot, dry places to very cold places and can survive in these because they go into a dormant dried-out form when necessary. Tardigrades are so resilient that when scientists sent some up into space, thereby exposing them to very low temperatures and radiation, they were still alive on return to Earth and able to lay viable eggs!

Fungi

Fungi may seem a bit like plants because they start life as a spore released by a mushroom or toadstool that then sprouts filaments (called hyphae) that look a bit like very fine roots, and these then form a branching network in the soil. Unlike plants, however, fungi do not have the green pigment chlorophyll, which is used in photosynthesis to obtain energy from sunlight, therefore they need a source of food (carbon). Their food source is organic matter and they are able to break down even very resilient organic compounds such as the lignin in wood. There are millions of different types of fungi and probably only about 5 per cent have been formally identified to date. One gramme of garden soil may contain 2km (1.2 miles) of fungal hyphae!

Fungus Structure

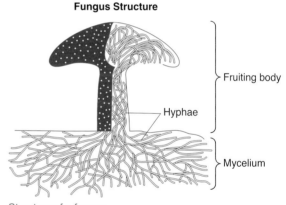

Structure of a fungus.

'White rot' fungi are the only organisms that can break down lignin, and their evolution is correlated with the end of the Carboniferous period, when dead plant material was accumulating on Earth (eventually forming coal).

Fungi release enzymes to break down large molecules into smaller ones that can be absorbed by the tips of the hyphae and moved to other parts of the fungus. The hyphae are thinner than plant roots so can explore much more of the soil than a plant's root system. Fungi compete with bacteria for some food sources and some are able to release antibiotics such as penicillium, which have been extracted for use by humans. The balance between fungi and bacteria in the soil has also been used as a soil health indicator.

Fungi are extremely important in the decomposition of organic matter once some of the larger animals have carried out the original shredding process. For this reason the number and range of species found is higher where there is a good supply of organic material. They are also more prevalent where soils are not disturbed because cultivation destroys their web of hyphae and they need to recolonize afterwards.

Ancient woodlands and forests have massive networks of fungi growing in the soil, connecting trees and helping them obtain nutrients from the soil in exchange for sugars released by the roots. The largest living land organism in the world is thought to be a honey fungus living under a forest in the Blue Mountains in Oregon, USA, measuring about 4km (2.5 miles) across.

Some soil fungi are damaging to plants, for example those causing root rots and club root. Perennial plants and trees can also be killed by a parasitic fungus in the Armillaria family known as honey fungus, which is very hard to eradicate so it may be necessary to grow trees/shrub species that are more resistant if it becomes a problem in your garden. The best way to avoid most fungal pathogens becoming a problem in vegetable plots and allotments is to rotate what you grow so that you do not grow the same crop in an area more often than once every four years. Adding compost regularly will also help because the general microbial population then increases and it becomes less easy for one species to run riot. Most fungi only feed on dead material, however, and do not harm trees. If you find fungi growing on your bark mulch or your compost heap, it is a saprophytic type and not harmful to your plants.

Fungi have a key role in forming soil aggregates because their hyphae act a bit like a mesh around soil particles.

Key Message for Gardeners

If you see toadstools in your lawn or beds, the fungus producing them is feeding on dead organic matter, and most types will not harm living plants.

Mycorrhizal Fungi

Some specialist soil fungi (called mycorrhizal fungi) form symbiotic relationships with plant roots. These are

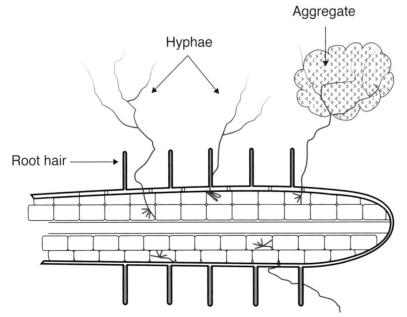

Root rhizosphere and mycorrhizal fungus.

particularly important for woody plants and trees because they increase the area of soil that can be exploited for nutrients and help the tree obtain sufficient nutrients and water as well as stabilizing soil aggregates.

In return for this, the plant releases exudates from its roots, which the mycorrhizal fungi feed on.

There are many species of mycorrhizae and around 80–90 per cent of all plant species form mycorrhizal associations.

Table 9 Types of mycorrhizae

	Characteristics	Plant examples
Ectomycorrhizae	Live outside the roots; nutrients can move between different plants in the same fungal network. Truffles are the fruiting bodies of one ectomycorrhizal fungus species	Around 10–20 per cent of tree species, for example oak, birch, pine, rose
Endomycorrhizae	Live within the root cell. Include vesicular arbuscular (VA) mycorrhizae, which are important for soil aggregate formation	Around 80 per cent of all herbaceous plant species

Mycorrhizae are especially important for phosphorus supply to woody plants and trees because most of the phosphorus in soils is not in a form that is available to plants. If you apply large amounts of phosphorus fertilizer to the soil you will effectively inhibit the growth of mycorrhizae because there is less incentive for plants to make associations with mycorrhizal fungi and give away some of the sugars they have made from photosynthesis. In the same way as other soil fungi, mycorrhizal fungi do not cope with soil disturbance, so do best in uncultivated areas.

Some species of plants do not form mycorrhizal associations and this includes many vegetable plants – cabbages, cauliflowers, broccoli, radishes, turnips, spinach, beet – and some flowers – dianthus, carnations, stonecrop. These plants are therefore more likely to need fertilizers containing phosphorus if the soil level is low.

It is possible to buy mycorrhizae innoculants to add to the soil when planting, but they need to be the correct type for the species you are growing and will only have a short shelf-life, so would only be viable if kept in optimum conditions after manufacture. Garden soil already contains a huge population of mycorrhizae so adding them artificially is only likely to be beneficial if the soil is of poor quality.

Nematodes

Nematodes are small, worm-like creatures around 0.5–1.5mm (0.02in–0.06in) long. Some are plant parasites, some feed on other nematodes and simple animals called protozoa, and some feed on bacteria. They can be damaging to plants, for example the potato cyst nematode, but some are used as biocontrol agents, for example to control vine weevil or slugs.

Protozoa

Protozoa are the simplest single-celled organisms, which come in many shapes and sizes. The type most people have heard of is an amoeba. Protozoa can only be seen under a microscope and mainly feed on bacteria within the water film around a soil particle. They all need moisture to live and some are parasitic – for example *Plasmodium*, which causes malaria. The soil contains millions of protozoa and the total mass of protozoa in a soil can be the same as the mass of earthworms.

Bacteria

Bacteria and virus are the smallest form of life in the soil. There are theories that the first life on Earth was Cyanobacteria (known as blue-green algae even though they are bacteria, not algae). It was the oxygen they released during photosynthesis that then accumulated in the atmosphere and allowed other organisms to evolve.

There are many different types of bacteria, but they are all single-celled and reproduce by dividing into two cells and then carrying on dividing. There are bacteria adapted to every type of environment on the Earth, from volcanoes to the depths of the oceans. Some bacteria need oxygen to respire in the same way as animals do, others can live in anaerobic conditions without oxygen. They cannot absorb large molecules of organic matter so they excrete enzymes to break them up into smaller nutrient ions that they can take in through their cell walls.

One gramme of soil may contain 10,000 different species, the highest concentration of bacteria being in the top 15cm (6in) of the soil, where there is more organic matter, with the largest population living in the area immediately around the plant roots, the rhizosphere. Bacteria live in the water-filled pores in the soil and can move towards sources of soluble carbon and away from adverse conditions. They carry out a wide range of functions, including making nutrients available to plants, and some can break down toxic pollutants in soil.

The bacteria in the soil are in a constant battle with other microbes as they compete for food sources. Antibiotics are the substances they produce to kill or inhibit the growth of other bacteria, and humans have been able to extract these from the soil to treat many bacterial diseases. Streptomycin is a widely used antibiotic that is produced by *Streptomyces*, which is in the Actinomycetes sub-group of bacteria, while other substances produced by soil bacteria are used as immunosuppressants following transplant surgery.

Clearly, soil is an extremely valuable resource for medicines.

The ratio of bacteria to fungi in a soil depends on what is growing in it and if it is being cultivated. Undisturbed soils under forests have a higher mass of fungi than bacteria because the fungal hyphae do not get destroyed by cultivation and those soils are naturally more acidic. Cultivated soils have more bacteria and less fungi. Generally speaking, the greater the number of different species of bacteria, the healthier the soil is.

Nitrogen-Fixing Bacteria

One particularly useful soil bacterium is called *Rhizobium* and this is the one that forms nodules on the roots of plants in the legume family (such as peas and beans), where nitrogen from the air is extracted and made into proteins. The nodules protect the bacteria and exclude oxygen, which is necessary because nitrogen fixation only occurs in anaerobic conditions. The plant provides the bacteria with food by releasing root exudates and in return it obtains nitrogen from the *Rhizobium*, which is essential for making proteins and other molecules.

Different species of *Rhizobium* are adapted to live in association with different leguminous plants, and it is possible to purchase seeds which have been treated with the appropriate species. If peas or beans are grown in a rotation in the vegetable plot, the *Rhizobium* will survive in the soil for several years between legume crops. The crop grown straight after peas or beans will benefit from any available nitrogen left in the soil, which is why crop rotations are one

Examples of Leguminous Plants

Peas
Beans
Clover
Wisteria
Lupins
Sweet peas
False indigo

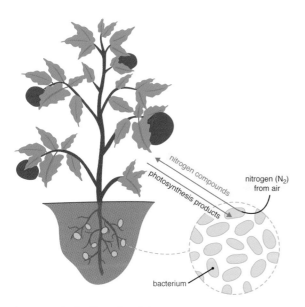

Legume plant with root nodules.

Leguminous plants form symbiotic relationships with specialized bacteria or fungi that form nodules on their roots and obtain sugars from the plant in exchange for nitrogen they extract from the air.

way of maintaining soil fertility with lower fertilizer inputs (although if you have harvested the peas or beans you will have removed much of the nitrogen in those). If large amounts of nitrogen fertilizer are applied to pea or bean plants, they won't form nodules because they don't need help with obtaining sufficient nitrogen.

There are other nitrogen-fixing bacteria that form associations with plant roots. Alder trees live in symbiosis with a bacterium called *Frankia*, which forms nodules on its roots in a similar way to *Rhizobium* and allows the alder trees to grow in nutrient-poor and waterlogged environments. Sea buckthorn also forms an association with *Frankia* so can establish itself on very poor, infertile soils.

In addition to these bacteria that have symbiotic relationships with plant roots, there are also free-living nitrogen-fixing bacteria in soils. These mostly feed on dead organic materials, and under anaerobic conditions they produce an enzyme that converts nitrogen gas into ammonia, which is then converted into other nitrogen compounds. Cyanobacteria belong to this group of bacteria. Free-living nitrogen-fixing bacteria are important in grass and cereal ecosystems.

Summary

- The life in the soil is essential for healthy plant growth: all plants depend on the soil ecosystem.
- The more biodiversity there is in the soil, the more healthy that soil is.
- Adding organic matter feeds the life in the soil, which will help you grow healthier plants.
- Minimizing soil disturbance is beneficial to both larger soil life forms such as earthworms and the smaller ones such as fungi.
- One of the most useful types of bacteria in the soil are the ones that form associations with the roots of leguminous plants, so these plants can obtain nitrogen from the air rather than relying on soil or fertilizer nitrogen.

CHAPTER 6

ASSESSING AND TESTING YOUR SOIL

There are a number of simple tests that we can do in our gardens to give us a better picture of the type of soil we have, its fertility and its health. In large garden areas, it may be that the soils are spilt into quite different types, but for many people the area will be small and only require a set of quick tests to determine some basic parameters. Simple things like adding organic matter and correcting soil acidity, if necessary, by liming can give big improvements in soil health and hence soil testing is particularly important for the gardener or allotment holder growing fruit or vegetable crops. Some soil tests can be done at home, others require sending soil samples off to a laboratory.

Table 10 Tests that are useful for gardeners

Test	Result	Ease of doing test	Alternative
Soil texture	Sands, silts or clays and the mixture of the basic particles	Very easy – finger-and-thumb test	Lab sieve test
Topsoil aggregate stability	Degree of slumping, an indication of the soil structure	Easy – soil aggregates in a saucer with water	Lab test
Soil organic matter (OM) content	The organic matter or humus content of the soil; measure of the food supply for soil life	Easy by observing colour of soil	Lab samples
Soil biological activity	Level of microbial activity in the soil measured by speed of breakdown of organic matter	Very easy 'tea bag test'	Lab test
Soil pH	Degree of acidity; potential need for lime application	Home test kits	Lab samples

(continued overleaf)

Table 10 *continued*

Soil nitrogen	N status	Home test kit	Lab samples
Soil phosphate	P status	Home test kit	Lab samples
Soil potassium	K status	Home test kit	Lab samples
Earthworm counts	Measure of soil health; influence on soil particle aggregation	Digging up soil and examining for earthworms	
Drainage status	To ascertain if there is a need to insert drains	Digging trial pits and seeing where the water table lies – plus soil colour	

Soil Texturing

Soil texture will fit into one of the main textural groups. Table 11 refers to the UK soil texturing system but similar ones are used in other countries. As already discussed, the basic soil texture group of your soil will have significant implications for how easy it is to manage, how droughty it will be, how well drained it may be and how well it holds onto plant nutrients. The ideal texture groups for gardeners or allotment holders wanting to grow a wide range of plants will be light loams, light silts, medium loams and medium silts. If you have one of the more extreme textures, however, it just means choosing plants that will be better adapted to those conditions and adding organic matter to make the soil more manageable.

To do a finger-and-thumb soil texture test is very straightforward:

1. Pick up a pinch of the soil you want to test.
2. Moisten the soil with a little water – enough to begin moulding the soil into a ball or sausage. You then start to sense the grittiness, soapiness or stickiness.

Table 11 Soil texture groups

Type	Characteristics	Symbol	Texture class
Sand	Feels gritty, lacks cohesion; loose when dry, not sticky when wet	S LS	Sand Loamy sand
Light loam	Feels slightly gritty, can be moulded when sufficiently moist but does not stick to fingers	SL SZL	Sandy loam Sandy silt loam
Light silt	Feels smooth and silky; can be formed into a ball that deforms easily	ZL	Silty loam
Medium loam	Moulds to form a strong ball when moistened and rolled in hand; may also feel gritty.	SCL CL	Sandy clay loam Clay loam
Medium silt	Moulds into a ball easily when moist; ball smears but does not take a polish when rubbed; feels silky and smooth	ZCL	Silty clay loam
Clay	Forms a ball easily that moulds like plasticine and can then take a polish when rubbed. Feels sticky when wet; may also feel gritty or smooth (sandy clay or silty clay)	SC C ZC	Sandy clay Clay Silty clay

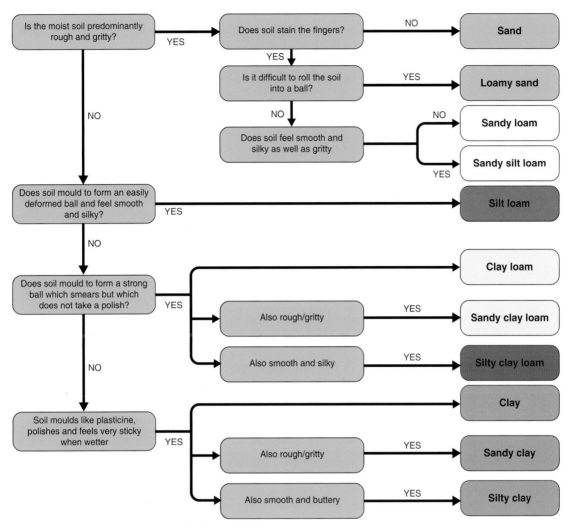

*Polish = Smooth shiny surfaces to soil when rubbed
Soil texturing flow chart.

If the soil is very much dominated by sand particles it will feel gritty (see Table 11). Where the soil is dominated by silt particles, such as river estuary deposits, then it will not be gritty (sands) or sticky (clays). While the silt soils can be rich in nutrients, the soil structural units are often very unstable and do not hold together, so soils that are highly silty easily slump and cap over (form a crust).

Topsoil Aggregate Stability

This is a very simple test and measures the combined effect of the texture of the soil, the organic matter

content and the degree of microbial activity. Soil organic matter feeds the microbes in the soil (see Chapter 4) and these secrete gums and waxes that stick the particles together.

1. Collect from the garden a sample of topsoil and spread the soil out to air dry, without crushing the soil structural units. Once dry, take the soil aggregates and place them in a saucer or bowl, then carefully add some water.
2. Record how quickly the soil aggregates break down when the water is added. Well-structured soils will take longer to break down than fragile ones.

Soil texture test, step 1: take a pinch of the soil you want to test.

Soil texture test, step 2: Once moistened, you can assess the texture of the sample.

Key Message for Gardeners

A soil with good a good 'crumb' structure with stable aggregates is less likely to cap over after heavy rain if the soil is left bare, but try to protect the soil surface on vegetable plots and allotments over winter by mulching.

Soil Biological Activity

A healthy soil will have a lot of microbial life, and these bugs will break down organic matter that is added to the soil. The greater the population of microbes (such as fungi and bacteria), the faster this breakdown will occur. One way of testing this is to carry out the 'tea bag test' (or the alternative cotton underpants test sometimes used by farmers!).

Tea Bag Test

Use tea bags that do not contain plastic.

1. Bury the tea bags in a few areas of the garden at a depth of 7–8cm (2.5–3in), marking the locations.
2. After ninety days dig up the tea bags.
3. If your soil has a good microbial population the tea bags should have almost decomposed.

Soil Tests for Nutrients

As suggested in Table 10, there are basically two ways we can easily test for the main nutrients in soils – home test kits and sending samples away to garden advisory services, such as that offered by the RHS Wisley.

Soil analysis is most likely to be useful for more intensively used growing areas, such as vegetable/fruit

Soil stability test, step 1: dry the sample out before rehydrating.

Soil stability test, step 2: time how long it takes for the sample to lose its structure.

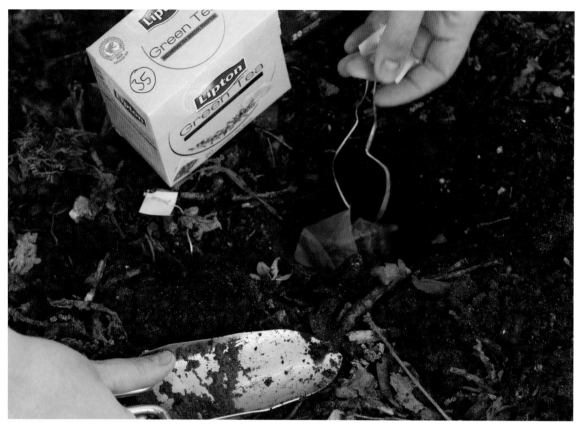

The 'tea bag test' is a simple way of assessing how much life there is in your soil. Make sure the tea bags used do not contain plastic, however!

gardens and allotments, where you want to make sure nutrient supply is adequate. There are numerous DIY test kits available; a typical kit is pictured here, but there is no suggestion that it is better or worse than any.

In all cases, the taking of the soil sample is the most important aspect of obtaining a meaningful result. For a small vegetable garden, a sample from just below the surface of the topsoil should be collected and merged with samples from a number of spots across the area. The only exception to this would be if there was a particular area of the garden where plants did not grow well and you wanted to see what the difference was between the good and poor areas. Then a number of samples from each area would be collected and tested against each other.

Once the samples are collected, they should be mixed as a bulk sample from each area and a smaller sample taken out as representative of the bulk for testing. The smaller sample should then be spread out to air dry before the tests are undertaken; most test kits would explain how to do this.

When soil samples are being sent off for testing, the sample collection is again critical and basically similar. The main difference, if sending a sample off for analysis, is that the soil does not need drying – the laboratory will oven dry the sample and grind it before analysing. Having said that, it is not advisable to sample the soil if it is very wet, as firstly the sample weight and volume will be dominated by water and secondly any available nutrients may well have been flushed out of the soil with recent rain.

Home Test Kits

The initial task is to collect the soil sample and prepare it for testing. The kit pictured here recommended taking sub-samples from a number of spots around

DIY soil test kits are available but results are generally less reliable than sending samples to a laboratory.

Soil needs to be mixed with water, shaken and allowed to settle before carrying out the tests on the solution.

the area requiring testing and mixing them, before extracting a sub-sample to be placed in a clean dish and allowed to air dry.

Once the sample was dried, it could be prepared for testing. This consisted of taking, on a volume basis, one part of the dried soil and adding four parts of water – the water recommended was rainwater or de-ionised water, such as used as a battery top-up fluid. Once the water was added, the sample vessel was capped and the sample shaken for thirty seconds and then left to settle; depending on the soil texture, this might take from thirty minutes to twenty-four hours. As a general guide, sandy soils will settle much more quickly that clayey or organic soils.

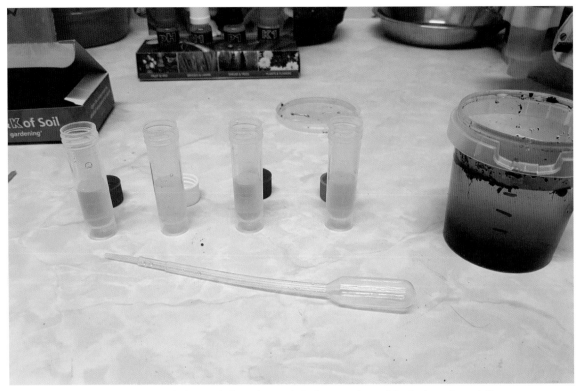

Soil needs to be mixed with water, shaken and allowed to settle before carrying out the tests on the solution.

In the case of this particular kit, a small pipette was supplied and allowed the nearly clear extracted solution to be drawn off the previously shaken, but now settled sample.

Each particular test (pH, N, P and K) had a colour-coded test tube and reagent bottle with a small paddle to add the dry reagent.

Each of the tubes had a sample of the clear liquid placed in it and then the reagents were added; the sample tubes were capped and then shaken and left to settle. The resultant colour development could then be compared with the charts in the handbook.

The results are easy to see but there are some aspects to consider:

pH – the indicator of acidity or alkalinity is very straightforward and the test kit used in this example gave a result which was not surprising – dark green, or 7.0+. Note that with pH scales running from green to red, anyone with red/green colour blindness may struggle to make the judgement needed.

Nitrogen Available nitrogen results are very difficult to interpret, especially after a wet winter period. The topsoil in any situation will often have been leached of available N and so the kit indicating a very low value is not surprising. The total nitrogen in organic material in the topsoil will be much higher but this will not be picked up by this test and will only become available to plants once microbes have broken down the organic matter (see Chapter 4). For vegetable growing, N fertilizer will often be needed to raise the available N level, but for flower borders the turnover of N from organic matter will usually be sufficient.

Phosphorus This is a complex element to estimate because P fertilizer added to soil tends to get bound up quickly into insoluble forms. In the case of the kit here, the results suggested a medium to low level. The type of extractant used in the kit will make a big difference to the result. Over the years many different laboratory techniques have been tried, and many countries have different extraction methods for P. Phosphorus ferti-

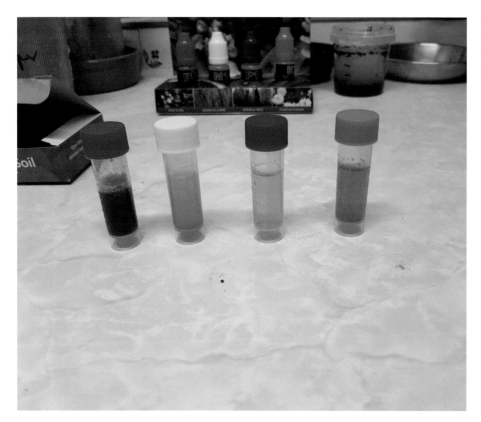

The colour of the solution can be compared with the charts provided.

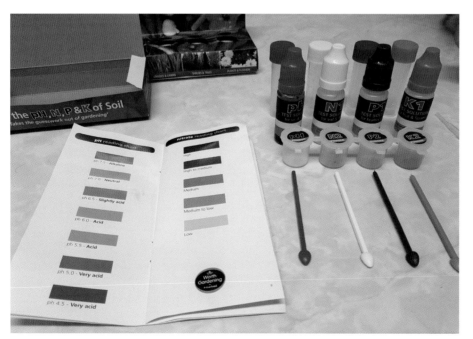

Home soil test results can be useful to check for nutrient deficiencies.

Using the pH indicator is a useful way to carry out a quick pH check. This soil has a pH of 7.

lizer is usually only needed if the soil P level is low and the soil will be used for vegetables/fruit, particularly potatoes. As discussed in Chapter 5, most plants use mycorrhizae to help obtain phosphorus from the soil.

Potassium The kit value for potassium (K) here suggested a medium level, which is probably near to a lab-based analysis. Potassium is quite soluble and levels can be maintained in clayey soils, but it is easily leached from sandy soils. If the soil level is low, potassium fertilizer will be beneficial for fruit and vegetable plots in particular.

Independent Laboratory Analysis of Soil Samples

There are a number of soil testing labs that offer gardeners an analytical service and, in some cases, specific fertilizer recommendations. In the case illustrated here, the author chose to send the sample to the Royal Horticultural Society (RHS) gardens at Wisley.

A similar soil sample to the one used for the home test kit was sent to the RHS, where they offer to obtain and report soil analysis results and give recommendations for specific use areas. Once you have applied online, you are sent the sample bags along with instructions for collecting the sample and providing the necessary details with regard to the origin of the sample and what you wish to have recommendations for – vegetables, flower beds, tree fruit and so on.

The results usually take about two to four weeks to come from sample submission, so obviously when planning for a coming season, the sampling really needs to be done either late autumn or very early in the new year.

While the recommendations from the report make reference to a base dressing of 'Growmore' (7-7-7 NPK), they also specifically guide the user to additional fertilizer inputs based on the crop type.

Royal
Horticultural
Society

Sharing the best in Gardening

Date Received	03-Mar-21
Date Reported	10-Mar-21

Laboratory Reference	
Sample Number	72707/513081/21

RHS Log No.	2377

Recommendations requested for :
Vegetables

Sample Name : VEG PATCH

SOIL ANALYSIS RESULTS

Soil Texture	Organic Sandy Clay Loam
Organic Matter	19.3 % (Very High)
Soil pH	7.1
Available Phosphorus	77.0 mg/l (Index 5, High)
Available Potassium	169 mg/l (Index 2, Medium)
Available Magnesium	194 mg/l (Index 4, High)

1. The provision of information by the RHS through its Soil Analysis Service to a subscriber is not an endorsement by the RHS of the competency, quality or otherwise of a subscriber to that service.

2. These results and recommendations are based entirely on the particular sample and information submitted. You are advised that to the fullest extent permitted by law we do not accept responsibility: firstly for any action other than those indicated in this report; secondly to anyone other than the subscriber to the RHS Soil Analysis Service for our results or recommendations or for the opinions we have formed.

rhs.org.uk

 /the_rhs   /rhshome

 INVESTORS IN PEOPLE

RHS Registered Charity No. 222879/SC038262.
Printed on 100 % recycled paper.

Summary of soil analysis results from RHS Wisley.

FERTILISER RECOMMENDATIONS

VEGETABLES

The level of organic matter measured in your soil was very high. Soils with very high levels of organic matter, or derived from peat have to be managed in a different fashion to normal mineral soils. Some peat soils are exceptionally acidic and have their own unique flora. These soils are best preserved in their natural state and remedial treatment is not advised. In a similar fashion, certain lowland peat soils are alkaline and have flora sensitive to those conditions. Again it is not advised to alter the pH of those soils by chemical methods.

Vegetables require a soil pH of about 6.5 for optimum growth. Different crops vary in their sensitivity to soil pH and under extremes of pH, restrictions to growth may occur.

Your soil pH was measured at 7.1. No lime is required this season. We suggest another soil test for pH is performed in the next 3 to 4 years.

Some soils have the ability to lock-up phosphorus, making a deficiency of this nutrient difficult to correct. To make best use of phosphorus fertiliser apply it so that it lies in close proximity to germinating seeds and young plants. Certain crops respond better to phosphorus containing fertilisers than others. Carrots, lettuce and spinach require high doses of phosphorus containing fertilisers whereas most of the cabbage family and parsnips have a lower requirement.

The level of available phosphorus measured in your soil is adequate for the majority of vegetables. A low level of phosphorus-containing fertiliser is required for crops that are considered to be sensitive to phosphorus deficiency such as carrots.

Potassium deficiency in vegetable crops generally occurs under intensive growing conditions where the demands for growth are high. It can also occur under conditions of drought and where high levels of other nutrients (for instance high levels of nitrogen fertiliser) have been applied. These deficiencies are corrected by regular fertiliser dressing but potassium is also released slowly from clay minerals breaking down in the soil.

The level of potassium in your soil is just about adequate for the cultivation of vegetables but some additional fertiliser would be beneficial. Where other soil nutrients are required, a general purpose base fertiliser can be used. Where little or no phosphorus and magnesium are required sulphate of potash could be used. Potassium containing fertilisers can be applied some weeks before sowing. However, the fertiliser must be thoroughly incorporated to reduce the risk of low germination rates and damage to the developing root system.

Accompanying notes interpret the results and are based upon the specific recommendation requested, in this case for vegetables.

The other result that comes with the report is the organic matter content. This obviously reflects the inputs to soil and also the likely stability of soil structural units. In the case of the soil tested here, it has had composted green waste (CGW) added to it over a number of years. The CGW was made up of various garden wastes, including grass clippings, and also all the green bin collection from the kitchen, including tea bags and coffee granules, and kitchen vegetable and salad waste. The CGW was either allowed to mature in large slatted wooden bins or in local authority-supplied 'rotter bins'

The soil organic matter level will normally be closely correlated with the amount of biological activity in the soil because it is the food source for soil microbes; it will also probably be linked to the number of earthworms.

A healthy soil will have an organic matter level of between 4 and 6 per cent but it will be hard to achieve this level with a sandy soil. Peat and fen soils will obviously have a higher level than this naturally.

'Rotter' compost bins are useful for making your own compost in smaller gardens.

Earthworm Activity and Counts

Usually, when digging in the early spring (March onwards in the UK), the soil in our vegetable patch is alive with deep-burrowing earthworms. The massive amount of organic matter in the top soil is a fabulous food for the worms, as it is full of both soluble nutrients and microbes, which the earthworms thrive on. If you dig too early in the year, you will not find worms near the cold surface soil but you may find them at around 30–50cm (12–20in), curled up in sealed soil chambers. Similarly, in very dry summer conditions, the worms will do the same, descending into the soil and then creating sealed chambers to survive in.

There are basically three type of worms that you will come across commonly in the garden (*see* Chapter 5):

Epigeic Brandling worms breed and digest the organic materials in the compost heap. These are also the bright-red worms much loved by fishermen.
Endogeic These very pale long worms live in the topsoil and burrow down to perhaps 40cm (15in). These worms often appear on the surface and move across rain-wetted surfaces after dry periods looking for a mate.

Anecic The very deep-burrowing *Lumbricus* worms are a dark reddish brown with familiar annular rings on the body. These create the best drainage pores in the soil and can easily burrow down to 1m (3ft) deep. They are excellent indicators of healthy, friable soils with good organic matter status.

The casts of earthworms are very rich in available nutrients, especially solubilized phosphates. Their constant activity in pulling down organic matter into the soil profile actually helps to avoid a 'thatch' building up on the soil surface. Some gardeners, who particularly pride themselves on the pristine nature of their lawns, will do everything possible to discourage and kill out earthworms as they do not like the earthworm casts on their lawns. This practice does not in fact help the lawn; instead it encourages the accumulation of organic matter as a mat at the soil surface, which then favours moss growth as the surface remains too wet.

Carrying out an Earthworm Count

Earthworm counts are best carried out in warm, wet conditions in spring or autumn.

There are three main earthworm types found in temperate climates such as the UK, living in different zones of the soil; the surface-dwelling ones are important for incorporating organic material into the soil, while the deeper-burrowing ones create soil pores.

Earthworm counts are not difficult to carry out but the soil needs to be moist, as earthworms migrate deeper into the soil under dry conditions.

1. Dig out a soil pit 20 × 20 × 20cm (8 × 8 × 8in) and place all the soil on a mat.
2. Carefully remove all the earthworms into a pot and count the number of adults (the ones with a saddle).
3. Return the earthworms to the pit and fill it back in.

An earthworm count of less than four is poor, four–eight is moderate and more than eight is good.

Drainage Status

General observations of how well your soil drains after rainfall and if surface ponding occurs are good indicators of the drainage status. The colour of the soil is also a good guide, as detailed in Chapter 2. There may be ways of improving this by adding organic matter and creating a better soil structure. If the poor drainage is due to groundwater levels rising over the winter there is not much that can be done, so the only way to achieve well-drained areas may be to build raised beds (*see* Chapter 7).

If the problem is slow movement of water from the upper layers of the soil into the deeper soil profile then a proper drainage system could be installed; this is an expensive option, however, and it is still important to improve the structure of a heavy clay soil so that excess water will flow into the drains.

Summary

- Soil testing is a good way of monitoring the health of your soil.
- Checking the soil pH and nutrient levels is more important for vegetable plots and allotments.
- Earthworm counts are easy to do and one of the best ways of assessing soil health.
- Increasing organic matter levels takes a while, so do not expect big changes in just a year or two; over time you will see a difference.
- Where soil testing shows a need, applying suitable fertilizers for specific crops is essential to achieve good growth and yields. The timing of fertilizer applications needs careful consideration.

CHAPTER 7

GROWING MEDIA FOR CONTAINERS

This chapter will cover the 'soil' (or growing medium) that is used for pots, hanging baskets, raised beds and other container growing systems. The different types of ingredients used to make a growing medium and their properties will be discussed and recommendations for choosing the most appropriate product for the intended use. In Europe, the types of growing media are changing because of the phasing out of the traditional ingredient, peat. This will mean gardeners

have to learn to manage container-grown plants slightly differently because new mixes will have different properties to media made with a large percentage of peat.

For most gardeners, it is best to use ready-made growing medium because it is not possible for the amateur gardener to obtain the same raw ingredients that are available to manufacturers. Specialist mixes, such as seed-sowing media, are particularly difficult to make at home. It is possible, however, to make your own potting mixes if you make your own good-quality garden compost and can obtain other materials to blend with this.

Although you might think of the contents of a raised bed or container as 'soil', its composition must be carefully considered to make sure it is suitable for the intended purpose. This type of soil is more accurately described as a 'growing medium', as it may contain some soil but often does not. It is unfortunate that in some countries the word 'compost' is used instead; this causes confusion because in most cases the material used has not actually been composted. The Dutch use the term 'potting soil', scientists may talk about 'substrate' and in some countries the term 'dirt' is used, but we will stick to 'growing medium'!

In a very large pot or raised bed, the growing medium will be closer to a true soil but in a smaller pot or hanging basket the major ingredients will not be

Why Grow Plants in Containers

More and more people are growing plants in containers or raised beds for a number of reasons:

- Plants can be grown in patio and courtyard areas without flower beds or borders.
- Raised beds can be used where the drainage is poor or soil quality is poor.
- Raised beds give easier access to plants for older and disabled gardeners.
- Plants not suited to the soil type in the garden can be grown in pots, e.g. acid-loving species.
- Even without any outdoor space, window boxes and hanging planters can be used to add colour and attract bees and other pollinating insects.

Large containers can contain woody plants as well as annuals and are less susceptible to drying out than small pots.

soil because the mix needs to hold more air and water than a typical soil for the plant to be able to survive with a restricted root system. Consider how far the roots of a plant or tree would spread if planted in a good soil and compare that to what you are giving it in a pot! An additional reason for not using garden soil in hanging baskets is the weight factor. Brackets for many baskets would not be strong enough if pure soil was used as the growing medium. Soil can weigh up to 1,200g/l (or 87lb/cu ft) while manufactured growing media usually weigh in between 300 and 600g/l (22–44lb/cu ft).

If you are growing plants in containers, it is important to remember that they will need to be watered regularly, often every day during hot and/or windy weather for smaller pots and hanging baskets. Even if you mulch the surface of the pot, the smaller volume of growing medium that the container plant root system has compared to a soil-grown one means that it will be more reliant on watering. If you want to reduce the time this takes, there are automatic irrigation systems available but these need to be maintained properly. It is a good idea to collect rainwater off roofs if possible – this will save money if you are on a water meter and is better for some types of plant if you live in a hard water area. However, if you are watering with rainwater, you may well need to feed extra calcium and magnesium to the plants. Check the fertilizer you buy to ensure that it supplies calcium and magnesium as well as the other major nutrients.

Constituents of Container Growing Media

In the UK and much of Europe, the major ingredient used to make growing media from the 1960s until recent years was peat. This is because peat was readily available, has many desirable properties and was cheaper than most alternatives. Many gardeners probably did not realize that multi-purpose compost and grow-bag products used to be pretty much just peat with fertilizer and lime added. In other parts of the world, where peat was not easy to get, such as Australia, materials such as bark have always been used as the basis of container growing media.

There have been concerns about the environmental impact of peat extraction for some time and there has been a gradual move away from reliance on peat over the last twenty years in the UK. This has been driven by concern over habitat loss, water storage and flood protection issues and, more recently, the fact that peat bogs are an immense storage reservoir of fixed carbon; once the bogs are drained and the peat removed, this not only prevents further storage but also releases the entrapped carbon into the atmosphere.

Most of the growing media products sold to gardeners have been 'peat-reduced' for quite a few years now but the move to growing media without any peat is going to require gardeners to rethink how they grow plants in containers, as the new blends will need different management. It also creates a challenge for the companies that make growing media because there is competition for wood-based materials from other industries, such as the renewable energy industry, and they need to be sure that products used to replace peat are sustainable.

The same issues relating to the physical and chemical properties of soil covered in chapters 2 and 3 are broadly applicable to a growing medium.

Physical Properties

In a container, the issue of the potting mix used holding enough air and water is even more critical because the plant root system has less volume to explore to obtain these. A growing medium therefore generally needs to have good air capacity but must also retain sufficient moisture so that the necessary watering interval is manageable. Generally speaking, the same model applies as already discussed for soil – large particles with large gaps between them hold more air and small particles packed more tightly together have small gaps, which hold more water. The particle size of a growing medium therefore has a similar influence on its properties as that of soil texture has on a soil.

The ideal mix will depend very much on the type/size of container and which plants are being grown. A 'multi-purpose' mix is quite a tall order when you consider the very different requirements of a medium for sowing seeds in, compared to one used to pot up a large shrub or tree. A growing medium for raising seedlings on the window sill or in a greenhouse will need to have small particles to hold sufficient water for the seeds to germinate, but if such a fine mix was used for a shrub outdoors it will get waterlogged over winter.

For a raised bed with a greater depth, the mix used to fill it will be more like a natural soil and it may be appropriate to use different material for the lower and top layers.

Key Message for Gardeners

Use a growing medium that is suitable for the plants being grown, bearing in mind that with peat-free products, a true multi-purpose product is not easy to achieve.

Most gardeners do not have the time or raw materials available to make up their own growing media, so are reliant on buying ready-to-use products from a garden centre.

It is important to choose the right product to suit what you are using it for. The main raw materials the manufacturers of these products are using are listed below.

Peat

This is being phased out and will feature less and less in the future. Graded peats do have a desirable blend of air- and water-holding capacity. Peat does, however, tend to stay wet on the surface, so moss and liverwort

Bedding plants are useful for instant colour for patios and courtyard gardens.

may colonize there; some types of peat are worse than others for encouraging this growth of moss and algae.

Wood Fibre

There are different types of wood fibre – some are natural by-products of forest operations and some are man-made. There are essentially three ways of producing man-made wood fibre:

Hammer milling, which produces chips in varying particle sizes depending on the type of mill
Mechanical extrusion between contra-rotating rollers
Expansion of woodchips with steam under high pressure

Each of these has different properties, but all wood fibres are much less retentive of water than peat, so need to be blended with other materials.

Bark

Bark used in container mixes is usually from coniferous trees because deciduous tree bark can contain plant toxins. There are basically two types of bark material

The use of peat in horticulture is being phased out for environmental reasons.

Natural and man-made wood fibres are increasingly being used in peat-free growing media.

used in growing media. Pine bark chips are naturally hard and are useful for creating air spaces in a growing medium so are often used in mixes for plants that need very good drainage, such as orchids. Composted bark fines are usually made from the bark of spruce, larch and western hemlock trees. This material, once composted, is much darker than pine bark and has a smaller particle size and a less granular structure.

Bark and woodchips are useful for improving drainage in growing media but may lock up nitrogen.

Coir

Coir is the pith extracted from the husk of coconuts, the other part of the husk being the fibre, which is mainly used for making rope and matting. It mostly comes from India, where it is also used as fuel for cooking, but because of its granular structure and free-flowing properties once dried and matured, it makes a good growing medium ingredient. The material is separated from the husks by soaking or milling and then laid out to dry in the sun. After turning and further drying, the pith is compressed into large blocks, which can be palletized and shipped. Re-wetting the blocks should yield three to four times the compressed block volume. Coir is used by many manufacturers and can be used on its own as it has good air- and water-holding properties, but it is expensive because of the shipping costs.

Green Compost

Green compost is the end product of composting green waste (and also sometimes food waste). Its properties have already been discussed in Chapter 4 because it is an excellent soil improver. Green compost used in a growing medium has to meet more rigorous standards, however, because any contamination or high nutrient level may be damaging to plants in containers. It is important to make sure any green compost used does not contain contaminants such as herbicide residues, or glass or metal shards.

UK Responsible Sourcing Scheme

In the UK, many manufacturers are now giving information on the bags of growing media about the percentage of peat they contain, and the sustainability of the ingredients used. All materials have some environmental costs in terms of their origin and their processing and transport requirements, so these have to be weighed up to formulate the most sustainable end product that still grows healthy plants and can be stored for a number of months before use. Manufacturers have to start making growing media for

Coir, a by-product from the coconut matting and rope industry, is a useful alternative to peat, with similar air- and water-holding properties.

Coir pith is then dried out in large piles.

The coconut husks are usually soaked and/or milled to separate the fibres from the coir pith.

Coir is compressed into bales for shipping and is then reconstituted before use in a growing medium.

Green compost can be used as a constituent of a growing medium but must be of good quality and is too nutrient-rich to be used undiluted, so is usually incorporated at a rate of up to 30 per cent by volume.

spring sales the previous autumn, so it is important that the products have a reasonable shelf life.

The Responsible Sourcing Scheme is being launched in the UK to help gardeners make informed decisions about the growing media they buy based on their environmental and social cost. The physical components used in growing media manufacture are being assessed against the same set of criteria:

Energy use – non-renewable energy used to extract, process and transport the material to the manufacturer. Some materials use a lot of energy to manufacture them (for example perlite), while others are transported long distances (for example some coir and some wood fibres).

Water use – potable water used in the processing of the material. This may be quite high for some materials such as coir.

Social compliance – this covers issues such as the working conditions for those employed when the product is manufactured.

Habitat and biodiversity – the impact of extracting/removing the material on the local environment as a habitat, especially if the biodiversity is reduced. Most peat scores badly for this because the peat bog is effectively destroyed by draining it. For forestry-derived products and coir, the types of plantation and how they are managed will affect the score for the material.

Pollution – any pollution occurring as a result of the extraction or processing of the material has to be recorded and will affect the score.

Renewability – this assesses how quickly a raw material can be replaced. A recycled product such as green compost scores very well; peat that takes thousands of years to form scores very poorly.

Resource use efficiency – this covers how much wastage occurs during the production of the raw material. Materials such as bark that are by-products of other industries score well for this.

In order to obtain a score against the criteria, data are collected for the individual ingredients and then the products they form part of can be scored. The scheme is independently audited, and the scores achieved by different products will be displayed on the bag for participating manufacturers.

Home-Made Growing Media

If you want to try to make your own potting mixes here are some guidelines:

- For a peat-free growing medium, coir is a good base, particularly if you want to use the mix for seed sowing, as it has good air- and water-holding properties and is low in nutrients. It can be bought in compressed blocks or bricks that you reconstitute by adding water.
- Granulated pine bark is useful to include at around 20 per cent if you need a well-drained mix for plants in pots that will be overwintered outdoors, for example azaleas or acers.

- Garden compost is a useful ingredient, but it must be mature and sieved to remove lumps and twigs. The compost must not contain lawn clippings from grass that has been treated with lawn weedkiller. Green compost has nutrients in it so cannot be used on its own – it must be diluted with lower-nutrient materials.
- Garden soil will contain a large amount of weed seeds so you will need to remove the weeds as they germinate. If it is cloddy or stony, it may need to be dried and sieved before use. It is also heavy and will reduce the aeration in the mix if more than about 20 per cent is used.
- For propagating cuttings, a very well-drained, low-nutrient mix is needed, so do not add garden soil or compost.
- Mature leaf mould (preferably more than two years old) can be included; sieve it for mixes for seeds and smaller pots.
- Unless it is a seed or cutting mix, you will need to add some fertilizer – the easiest way is to add controlled-release fertilizer granules, which can be done at potting by adding it as you fill the pot. A rate of 2–4g/l depending on the size/age of plants being grown is needed – this equates to approximately half a teaspoon for small (9cm/3.5in pots), and one teaspoon per litre for larger pots.

Raised Beds

Creating raised beds is a useful option if the soil in your garden is very poor quality or prone to flooding. They are also more accessible to gardeners who are physically challenged. Raised beds can be used for flowers or vegetables, but if you want to grow root crops such as potatoes they need to be at least 40cm (15in) deep.

Because raised beds are well drained and above natural ground level, the growing medium in them will tend to warm up a bit quicker in the spring, which is beneficial when growing early salad or vegetable crops. They can also be covered with glass or polythene to give frost protection early in the year. When filling a raised bed, the aim is to create a profile similar to that of a natural soil. Coarser, well-drained material should be used at the base as a 'subsoil' with a 'topsoil' of finer grade overlying this. The lower layer could contain more garden compost or bought-in green compost, mixed with garden soil. Top up with a

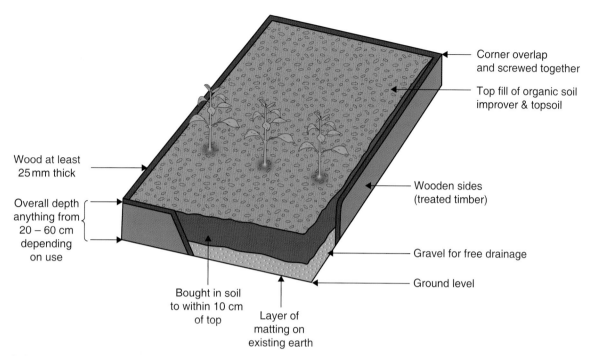

Corner overlap
and screwed together

Top fill of organic soil
improver & topsoil

Wooden sides
(treated timber)

Gravel for free drainage

Ground level

Wood at least
25 mm thick

Overall depth
anything from
20 – 60 cm
depending
on use

Bought in soil
to within 10 cm
of top

Layer of
matting on
existing earth

Raised bed construction and layers.

blend of garden soil and organic material such as compost or leaf mould or bought peat-free growing medium.

If the raised bed is filled just with bagged multi-purpose compost this will tend to slump over time.

Feeding Plants in Containers

The restricted root zone in a container system means plant roots have less area to explore to find nutrients and are more reliant on the use of fertilizers to sustain them, particularly food crops such as tomatoes and vegetable plants in raised beds.

Even if you purchase a ready to use mix to fill tubs and hanging baskets, most products only contain enough fertilizer to last for a month or two, so if you want the plants to continue to grow well they need feeding.

The two options for this are either adding controlled-release fertilizer granules when you pot up or feeding once a week during the growing season with a liquid feed.

Controlled-release fertilizers are ideal for providing nutrients for the whole season in containers/hanging baskets.

Hanging baskets are good for instant colour but require a reasonably moisture-retentive mix and regular watering in dry weather. Adding controlled-release fertilizer granules will save having to apply liquid feed.

Starved plants appear yellow and stunted in growth; once plants are very starved it will take several weeks of feeding to correct this.

The advantage of the controlled-release granules is they will provide nutrients for the whole summer, and for 'greedy' plants, such as hanging baskets, it saves a lot of time. For long-term plants in containers you can then just add some more the following spring to top up.

There are many specific formulations of liquid feed for different plants, but a general tomato feed will be fine for most flowering plants and fruit/vegetables in containers. This will have plenty of nitrogen for general plant vigour but also a good level of potassium, which is needed for flower and fruit development. Fast-growing plants such as tomatoes may need feeding at every watering, while tubs may only need a feed once a week. If the plants are looking pale and lacking in vigour, they may be lacking in nutrients.

Summary

- Plants in pots/containers need a growing medium with a higher air content than garden soil.
- It is usually better to buy in ready-to-use growing media, but you can make your own.
- The growing medium used should be appropriate for the type of plants to be grown and the container; for example, are you sowing seeds in a patio container or growing vegetables in a raised bed?
- Plants in containers have restricted root systems so will need feeding.
- Newer peat-free growing media will need different management to traditional peat mixes – probably more 'little and often' watering.

CHAPTER 8

SIMPLE WAYS TO IMPROVE SOIL HEALTH

From the earlier chapters it will be clear that the most important thing is to really understand the soil you have in your garden or allotment. Several questions need to be considered:

1. Is the garden you have founded on brand new (maybe imported) soil or is it soil that has been around the property for many years?
2. Have you defined the soil type and texture?
3. Is the soil waterlogged or does it flood?
4. What is the organic matter status of the soil?
5. Is there evidence of plenty of earthworm activity?
6. Have you had the soil pH tested?
7. Have you applied garden compost to your garden? Do you use commercial soil improvers?

Investigating your local geology and using the tests suggested in Chapter 6 will help to answer these questions, which will tell you a lot about the soil you have and can indicate routes to improving the soil health.

Things to Consider about your Soil

The Influence of Soil Texture

Knowing the texture of your soil is very useful when learning how to manage it. In general terms, people talk of light (sandy) soils, medium (loamy) soils and heavy (clayey) soils. The texturing of the soil (Chapter 6) determines which of these broad categories the soil falls into and gives valuable information about how the soil will behave and how best to improve it.

Light soils generally do not hold water or nutrients and their structure is often very poor, but they do have the advantage of warming up quicker in the spring and being well drained so can be beneficial for early vegetable crops, such as lettuce or early root crops, provided irrigation is available. Lawns on light soils will be susceptible to drought in dry summers but will recover in the autumn. Light soils in borders will benefit from mulching to retain soil moisture, especially for plants such as roses that need a good water supply. They are more suited to growing plants adapted to dry summers, for example Mediterranean species such as lavender.

Medium soils are the most forgiving, but even these soils can be improved by the addition of organic matter, which not only helps to stabilize the soil structure but improves the water and nutrient retention. The best time to apply organic matter to all soils is the autumn, as firstly the soil is still warm and hence the biological activity is high, and secondly to avoid the incorporation of the organic matter competing for available nutrients during its breakdown and hence robbing plants in the spring of easily available nutrients.

Heavy soils are often wetter for longer and colder in the spring period, so are fine for borders or lawns but less easy to manage for cultivated areas and allotments. They will hold onto nutrients and water but these may not easily be available to the plants. Again, the introduction of organic matter into the soils helps and the encouragement of earthworms will ensure that organic matter gets incorporated and new drainage channels are formed as the earthworms burrow into the soil.

Poorly Drained Soil

The drainage status of the soil is very important; if the soil drains poorly, organic matter cannot be fully broken down and incorporated into the soil profile because there is a lack of oxygen. Plant roots are subjected to root-rotting diseases and are killed, and earthworm activity is discouraged. The soil can become stagnant (and smelly!), very much like bad eggs.

If the soil is waterlogged due to a naturally high water table all year round then there is not much that can be done except to work with it and create a wetland garden. In other cases, a drainage system may help, or the use of gravel-filled slots ('French drains') to move surface water away. A full drainage system will be expensive and needs to be designed by a professional drainage engineer.

If the poor drainage is just the result of compaction, it may well be possible to improve it by loosening the soil when dry enough and adding organic matter.

Poor Soil Structure and Low Organic Matter

If your garden or allotment is on ex-arable farmland, it may be low in organic matter because arable cropping, where crop residues such as straw are removed, and minimal inputs of organic material can gradually reduce soil carbon.

The key to healthier soils is raising the humus level. More woody materials, such as green compost or your own garden compost, will give a longer-term slow-release supply of organic matter than straw-based manures. It is a slow process, so do not expect to see instant results, but over a few years the soil should gradually start to look darker and more friable and earthworm numbers should increase. Water- and nutrient-holding will be improved too, so it is well worth the investment, especially as drier summers seem to be more normal in many areas now.

A well-structured soil will not benefit from double digging or rotavating – all that will do is reduce valuable soil carbon and destroy the homes and refuges of the soil life that we need to encourage, from fungi through to earthworms.

Soil Acidity

As discussed in Chapter 1, soils formed over certain rock types, such as sandstones, naturally have a low pH, but even heavier clay soils can become acidic if they have not been limed. The dramatic effect this has on nutrient availability means that maintaining the correct pH is particularly important for vegetable gardens and allotments. Some crops are especially sensitive to acidity – for example lettuce, peas, beans, celery and the cabbage family; the latter are more susceptible to club root in low pH soils. Correcting acidity is one of the simplest ways of improving your soil if you are trying to grow your own fruit and vegetables.

The soil pH is very easy to check (*see* Chapter 6), and this should be done every few years unless you have naturally chalky soil. Aim to maintain it at around 6.5–7.0 for vegetables; other plants, such as fruit plants, many shrubs and grass, will be fine at a slightly lower level and you only need to be concerned if the pH is below 6.0.

If you have naturally acid soil it makes more sense to cultivate plants that are adapted to this for much of the garden, for example rhododendrons, camellias and azaleas, and just add lime to any vegetable-growing areas.

Examples of Soil Problems and Remedial Actions

This section looks at examples of the types of soil issues you may encounter and what might be done to address them.

New-Build Garden

If the answer to question 1 at the start of this chapter is that the garden is brand new, then the imported topsoil may not have any continuity with the subsoil or rock it is sitting upon. Effectively you may well regard the soil as being a 'container' of 30–40cm (12–16in)

Soil Data

Location of garden: Shropshire, UK
Soil series: Unknown imported topsoil
Soil type: Sandy loam
Soil structure: Compacted at 30cm (12in)
Drainage: Poor in places
Earthworm count: 1

New-build gardens may look great when first landscaped, but plants will often suffer once stressed by drought in their first summer or poor drainage over winter. Adding organic matter will help in the establishment phase.

deep, and the underlying layers will for years have very little influence on your topsoil. In this case there is certainly no point in deep digging; as long as the garden does not have free-standing water on it then growing any plant in the soil should be done using minimum cultivation. Simply plant into the soil and ensure that the plants are not allowed to dry out. If you are going for deeper-rooting plants, such as trees, it will be very important to dig large planting pits and try to break up any compaction at depth from when the site was trafficked by heavy machinery.

In a new-build garden the most common cause of plant death is either drought in the first couple of summers because plants were not able to root deeply and watering was insufficient or waterlogging over winter due to compaction. Over time, the plant roots themselves will help to form soil structure, and adding organic matter will help to get the soil biology working for you.

Small Garden on Poorly Drained Clay

Soil Data

Location of garden: Surrey, UK
Soil series: Wickham
Soil type: Clay loam
Soil structure: Good in lawn area, poorer in beds
Drainage: Poor, waterlogging at lower end of garden
Earthworm count: 4

Young fruit trees in raised beds will do better if the natural drainage is poor; adding compost as a mulch will also help.

The drainage status of the soil is very important; in poorly drained soils, organic matter cannot be fully broken down because there is a lack of oxygen, plant roots are killed and earthworms are discouraged. The soil can become stagnant (and smelly). A drainage system or the use of gravel-filled slots ('French drains') would help to move surface water away; in this case, however, a full drainage system was considered to be too expensive because it would need to be designed and installed by professional drainage engineers.

In some areas the poor drainage was just the result of soil compaction and it was improved by loosening it when dry enough and adding organic matter. Good-quality (PAS100 certified) 10mm green compost was bought in large bulk bags and used to mix into beds and as a mulch on the vegetable patch over winter. A coarser grade, more woody green compost was used as a mulch around fruit trees and newly planted shrubs. This compost will help to raise the organic matter level in the soil and the earthworm count increased to six within three months.

At the end of the garden, where the soil was wet-test, a raised bed area was created to grow some small fruit trees.

Large Garden on Ex-Arable Land

Compacted ex-arable topsoil can be a challenge for a new garden; again, adding organic matter will improve the soil quality.

Soil Data

Location of garden: Oxfordshire, UK
Soil series: Denchworth
Soil type: Clay loam, stony
Soil structure: Poor, compacted during contouring of site
Drainage: Poor in some areas
Earthworm count: 3

If your garden or allotment is on ex-arable farmland, it may be low in organic matter because crop residues such as straw are sometimes removed and there are few inputs of organic material; this gradually reduces the soil carbon level over time.

This garden in Oxfordshire was being planted on land that was previously part of an arable field. Unfortunately, the soil was moved to create the desired contours when it was wet, and this damaged the soil structure even further.

The key to healthier soils is raising the humus level, and the recommendation here was to add green compost and mushroom compost to achieve this. More woody materials, such as green compost or garden compost, will give a longer-term slow-release supply of organic matter than straw-based manures or mushroom compost.

Garden on Chalk

Soil Data

Location of garden: Kent, UK
Soil series: Coombe
Soil type: Shallow chalk
Soil structure: Satisfactory
Drainage: Good
Earthworm count: 6

The main problem in this garden was the naturally free-draining soil causing plant loss in dry summers. Shallow soils over chalk or sand are susceptible to drought in dry summers – keeping the soil covered to reduce moisture loss will help. The soil depth was gradually increased by adding organic matter as a

Chalk soils are shallow and not suitable for plants that need moisture-retentive conditions or plants that need acid soil, but larger shrubs and trees will root into the fissures in the chalk over time.

mulch every autumn/winter. The mulch was a mixture of home-made garden compost using prunings, lawn clippings and leaf mould.

The planting was also adapted to avoid species that would be heavily reliant on watering during dry weather and using more herbaceous and Mediterranean plants that cope with low rainfall in summer.

Allotment on Clay Loam Soil

Soil Data

Location of allotment: Leicestershire, UK
Soil series: Wick
Soil type: Clay loam
Soil structure: Poor in some areas
Drainage: Poor
Earthworm count: 5

This allotment had poor soil structure due to low organic matter and low biological activity because of this. The previous occupier had also been over-zealous in the application of slug pellets!

The new tenant had to first get rid of perennial weeds, so they mulched with cardboard and a 20cm (8in) layer of compost for the first year. This significantly

Allotments growing fruit and vegetables need regular applications of organic material and checks on the pH and nutrient levels.

weakened growth of weeds such as bindweed, with any shoots being removed as soon as they appeared. Another 5cm (2in) of mulch was then applied annually in the autumn after harvest of summer crops or early spring after winter cabbage and so on had finished.

The soil structure after three years was much improved and the soil much darker in colour due to the higher organic matter content. The worm count had increased to nine and the drainage over winter was much improved.

Summary

- Research your local soil types and find out as much as possible about the soil in your garden or allotment.

- Carry out some simple tests to check the health of your soil. More detailed analysis may be needed to diagnose problems or for intensively used allotments.
- The answer to many soil problems is raising organic matter levels to encourage earthworms and other soil life. This will improve the health of both light and heavy soils.
- Once you have achieved a reasonable soil structure, minimize disturbance of the soil and let nature do the work for you!
- Use mulches not muscle power to deal with weed problems in your soil.

GLOSSARY

Acidic A high hydrogen ion concentration in the soil (low pH)

Aerobic conditions Conditions in which oxygen is available

Aggregates Clumps of soil particles

Air capacity The amount of air the soil can hold

Alkaline A low hydrogen ion concentration in the soil (high pH)

Alluvial soils Soils formed in deposits by surface water, near rivers, floodplains and deltas

Anaerobic conditions The conditions experienced once all the available oxygen is used up. Some microbes can operate in an anaerobic environment but many need oxygen

Available water Water in the soil that plant roots are able to take up

Bacteria Microscopic living organisms, usually only consisting of one cell

Biodiversity The biological variety and variability of life on Earth

Biosequestration The net removal of carbon dioxide from the atmosphere by plants and microbes and the storage of the carbon in vegetation and soils

Biota The animal and plant life of a particular habitat

Buffering capacity The ability of a soil to hold onto and release nutrients into the soil solution

Carbon cycle The process by which carbon moves from the atmosphere into living creatures and then back

Chlorophyll A molecule that absorbs sunlight and uses the energy from it to make carbohydrates from carbon dioxide and water

Chlorosis Loss of the normal green colouration of leaves

Coir A growing medium ingredient derived from the husks of coconuts

Compost The end product after the composting (managed decomposition) of organic materials

Controlled-release fertilizers These are generally resin or polymer encapsulated granules of fertilizer. The release of the nutrients from such fertilizers is moisture and temperature dependent. There are different longevities available

Decomposition The breakdown of complex molecules into simple ones

Electrical conductivity A measure of the amount of dissolved nutrients or salts in the soil or growing medium solution

Enzyme A chemical that speeds up or facilitates a chemical reaction

Erosion The processes associated with water, wind, fluctuating temperatures and ice, which wear away rocks and or soils

Fungi A group of living organisms that are neither animals nor plants; includes mushrooms, toadstools, yeasts and moulds

Geosmin The chemical that gives damp soil its characteristic earthy smell

Gleyed colours A soil science term for the blue-grey colours associated with waterlogged soils

Green compost The end product of composting plant residues

Growing medium A material used to grow plants in a container or contained bed

Humic compounds Partially stabilized breakdown products from organic materials; they tend to give the warm brown colours to soils

Immobilization The process in which inorganic nutrients are taken up by microbes in the soil and converted into organic form as part of their bodies; the nutrients are not then available to plants

Inorganic Not consisting of or deriving from living matter

Ion An atom or molecule with a net electric charge due to the loss or gain of one or more electrons

Macrobiota Larger soil organisms, such as insects and earthworms

Mesobiota Organisms generally ranging from 0.1 to 2mm in size, for example nematodes

Metabolite A substance, usually small molecules, made or used when complex molecules are broken down to produce energy

Microbe/micro-organism Very small plant or animal organism that cannot be seen with the naked eye

Microbiota Microscopic soil creatures, such as bacteria and fungi

Mineralization The process by which the nutrients in organic compounds are released during decomposition in soluble inorganic forms, which may be available to plants; the opposite of immobilization

Molecule A group of atoms bonded together; the smallest unit of a chemical compound

Moraine The rock and soil debris left after glaciation

Mulch A material used as a layer on the surface of the soil primarily to retain soil moisture and suppress weed growth

Mycorrhizal fungi Extremely ancient fungi that freely coat and invade higher plant root systems, establishing a symbiotic relationship that helps to feed soluble nutrients to the plant in exchange for organic food compounds from the plant

Nitrogen cycle The process by which nitrogen gas in the atmosphere is made available for plant growth by being converted into different forms

Nitrogen fixation process by which free-living microbes in the soil and/or specific bacteria that form nodules on the plants' roots draw in and fix atmospheric nitrogen and help to form complex protein compounds

Organic A substance that contains carbon that is/was part of a living organism

Organic fertilizers Fertilizers that are either plant- or animal-based or both. Organic fertilizers are slow release as they have to be processed in the soil by microbes in a process called mineralization

Organic matter Dead plant, animal, manure or microbe remains

Parent material The rock or sediment that a soil is formed from

pH A measure of the degree of acidity or alkalinity of materials. The scale runs from 1 to 14, with 7 being neutral; from 7 down to 1 is increasing acidity and 7 to 14 is increasing alkalinity

Photosynthesis The process by which plants use energy from sunlight to convert carbon dioxide and water into sugars

Plant nutrients The various chemical elements, such as nitrogen (N), phosphorus (P) and iron (Fe), that are essential to plant growth.

Regenerative system A system that improves health of the soil; a conservation and rehabilitation approach to food and farming systems, increasing biodiversity, improving the water cycle, supporting biosequestration and increasing resilience to climate change

Respiration The way that energy is released from sugar (glucose) to power all the chemical processes in living cells

Rhizosphere The few millimetres of soil around the plant roots in which the chemical and microbial activity is influenced by the root growth, respiration and nutrient exchange

Soil horizon A distinct layer of soil within the soil profile

Soil improver A material, usually organic matter, used to improve soil health and fertility

Soil profile The different layers of the soil, from the surface to the underlying rock

Soil structure The way soil is aggregated into units with air spaces/cracks in between them

Soil texture The proportion of sand, silt and clay in a soil

Stomata Cell structures in the epidermis (outer layer) of plant leaves that are involved in the exchange of carbon dioxide and water between plants and the atmosphere

Tilth The physical condition of the soil as it relates to plant growth; the state of aggregation of a soil

Transpiration The process of water movement through a plant and evaporation from its aerial parts

Water-holding capacity The amount of water that a soil can hold; the *available* water holding capacity is a more useful variable (the amount of water held by a soil or growing medium that a plant can extract)

Weathering The processes of erosion that affect all rocks and lead to the breakdown of the initial material into finer and finer end products

Wood fibre A growing medium ingredient derived from wood, either naturally produced as a forestry by-product or man-made by processing woodchips

INDEX